Cigarette Cards and Novelties

Frank Doggett

Cigarette Cards and Novelties

Michael Joseph

A simple price code has been used to give the reader
a guide as to the retail price of sets, in good
condition, at the time of publication. The letters
indicate the price range shown, and have been placed
after the issue date in the captions to illustrations.

A Under £5
B £5 to £20
C £20 to £50
D £50 to £100
E Over £100

First published in Great Britain in 1981 by
Michael Joseph Ltd
44 Bedford Square, London WC1B 3DU

Cigarette Cards and Novelties
was edited and designed by
Prospect Publishing Co Ltd
1 Station Parade, Kew Gardens, Surrey
Editor: Oliver Freeman

© 1981 Prospect Publishing Co Ltd

Printed and Bound in Hong Kong by
South China Printing Company

ISBN 0 7181 1970 3

Contents

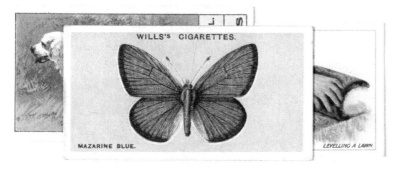

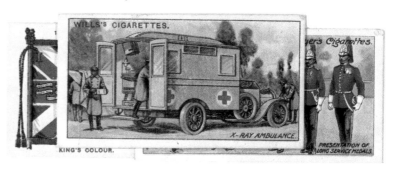

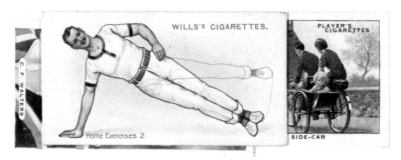

Historical Introduction

Sir Walter Raleigh observed that the natives of America burned the leaves of the tobacco plant for the soothing fragrance of its smoke, and when he returned to England he brought with him a quantity of the weed for the Court of Queen Elizabeth. As trade with North America developed, so did the tobacco habit. At first it was just a diversion for the rich, but gradually tobacco became an everyday commodity enjoyed by the masses. It was a slow process which matched the tempo of life in those days. It was a time when the great majority of the populace lived in villages and relied upon the land for a living. Towns were largely market places for agricultural produce. Industry and commerce were on a small scale, there were no newspapers, and the only way that tradesmen could advertise was by word of mouth or by crudely printed hand bills.

By the end of the eighteenth century, times were changing. The art of printing had advanced, the first daily paper was being published, and tradesmen were commissioning properly engraved cards to hand out to customers acclaiming their goods and services. The harnessing of steampower led to the growth of industrial towns centred on the coalfields on both sides of the Atlantic. The new generation of urban-dwellers, drawn from depressed rural areas by the prospect of work, were in alien surroundings, their lives were drab and they themselves were at best semiliterate. Here then was the ideal environment in which colourful cards would have an impact, and tobacco was the kind of product which was best distributed ready-wrapped with some form of internal stiffening to protect the contents. It was these factors

OGDEN'S CIGARETTES.

SIR WALTER RALEIGH.

which led to the introduction of cigarette cards, but their precise origins are difficult to track down.

It is known that the earliest cards were issued in North America, and that they were well established by the 1880s. The original cards were probably produced in the preceding decade, but the lack of material and the problem of dating that which is available means that painstaking research is needed to determine which card was the first, assuming of course that it is still in existence.

Until recently, the oldest card to be accurately dated was one depicting the Marquis of Lorne, a Governor-General of Canada. It is referred to in a publication circulated in 1879. However, a study of the Burdick Collection of early tobacco advertising material in the Metropolitan Museum of Art in New York has revealed a tobacco card dating from around 1877. This is a large card issued by R.C. Brown, maker of 'Capadura' Cigars, and the picture shows a top-hatted gentleman holding a card inscribed '1877'. At the bottom of the card is the caption 'Happy New Year' implying that the card was issued in 1877, or even 1876, and from its size (145 × 63 mm) it was probably inserted in a cigar box. But only 'probably'. It is difficult, often impossible, with these larger cards, to distinguish with any certainty between those which were inserted inside packages, those which were handed out with the product, and those which were distributed by tobacconists as promotional material not directly connected with the sale of a particular line. Nevertheless, the true cigarette cards are those which were actually supplied inside the packet.

The earliest cards were singles rather than parts of a series on a common theme. The series idea was a logical progression based on the principle that if a smoker found one card attractive, more cards on the same subject would be an encouragement to him to continue buying the product in order to collect the whole range. His enthusiasm would motivate him to persuade friends or colleagues to do the same, so that he could exchange duplicates and thus build up a set more easily. And so the hobby of card collecting or cartophily was born.

Development

The success of the early series led other firms to adopt this comparatively inexpensive sales aid. The spread of colour lithography and the mechanisation of printing enabled high-quality cards to be run off by the million. Well-known artists were commissioned by the larger companies which set up their own special departments to deal with the production of new series. Companies such as Allen & Ginter, Duke, Goodwin, Kimball, Kinney, Lorillard and Mayo were among the more active issuers at this period in the 1880s. The backs of the cards rarely had any descriptive text and the most popular subjects were actresses, beauties, animals, birds, flags, and sportsmen, reflecting their origins with their American emphasis. There were also several series produced on specifically American topics such as baseball, US Presidents, trotting, cowboy scenes, great Americans, US industries, State Governors, and Indian Chiefs. One of these American companies, Allen & Ginter, introduced cigarette cards to Britain, by packing with their Richmond Gem cigarettes a pair of oval cards held together by a stud, one

section of which comprised a calendar for 1884 with UK parcel postage rates on the back.

British tobacco manufacturers were aware of the effect that cards had been having on the American market, and the long established Bristol firm of W.D. & H.O. Wills was the first actually to produce cards in this country, around 1888; but factual information is hard to come by. Their printers, Mardon, Son and Hall, are thought to have run off a type-set card in two colours for Wills in 1887, although no specimens are known to be in existence. In the following year, it is believed the same firm produced at least four different paper-thin cards. The fronts showed a picture of a packet of ten Wills cigarettes, Gold Flake, Best Birds Eye, Dubec or the The Three Castles, with an advertisement on the back listing fourteen cigarette brands but excluding 'Woodbine' and 'Cinderella' cigarettes which are known to have been introduced in 1888. Over the next few years Wills issued several more advertisement cards and the Nottingham firm of John Player and Sons followed suit. These two companies were the first in this country to circulate planned series of cards and, during the years leading up to the end of the century, beautifully printed cards on ships, soldiers, cricketers, kings and queens, builders of the empire, conundrums, seaside resorts and the Transvaal were issued by Wills, whilst Players concentrated on beauties, actors and actresses, and four series with a military theme. Other tobacco manufacturers joined their ranks. Of these, Ogdens of Liverpool were probably the biggest.

WILLS
KINGS & QUEENS 1902 C
SET OF 50
The complete set value shown is for the set where
'Wills' is printed at the base. A second series
was issued with 'Wills' at the top.

WILLS
BUILDERS OF THE EMPIRE 1898 D
SET OF 50

In 1894 Ogdens introduced their 'Guinea Gold' brand of cigarettes and during the course of the next thirteen years photographic cards covering many thousands of different subjects were issued under the 'Guinea Gold' or 'Tabs' banner. Prior to that period, photography had been in its infancy, although the medium had been used to a limited extent for certain card issues in the USA during the 1880s. The Guinea Gold cards give a fascinating insight into life around the turn of the century. Personalities of the day, politicians, war leaders, royalty, sportsmen, stage artists, musicians, authors, artists, ships, motor cars, trains, horses, were all depicted. In fact almost every facet of those times is faithfully recorded, and luckily, because Ogdens were such prolific issuers, these cards are still commonplace to this very day. Ogdens were the first company to recognise the enormous potential of photographs as a means of attracting smokers to their brands, and even advertised that their cigarettes should not be accepted without the photo in the packet. The success of their policy is reflected by the fact that the company expanded from its modest origins in 1860 to become one of the biggest manufacturers in 1900 when they had the capacity to turn out something like 900 million cigarettes a year. It was at this time that the 'Tobacco War' broke out, and the firm of Ogdens was at the centre of the conflict.

The seeds of the Tobacco War were sown in 1890 when James 'Buck' Duke, head of the US Company, W. Duke Sons & Co, which had already swallowed up some two hundred small independent firms in the USA, masterminded the merger of

several large tobacco manufacturers to form the giant American Tobacco Company. Duke then turned his attention to the lucrative British market, but, because import duty on processed tobacco goods was considerably higher than that on raw tobacco, American-made cigarettes were much more expensive and could not compete with the home product. So he decided to acquire an English factory and, when his efforts to purchase John Player and Sons Ltd failed, he settled for Ogdens at a price of five million dollars, the deal being completed in September 1901.

The British manufacturers recognised the danger and moved fast. Directors of thirteen of the largest companies held a council of war in Birmingham on 19 September, when they decided to pool their resources in an all-out effort to beat the American invasion. As a result of this meeting the Imperial Tobacco Company was set up under the Chairmanship of Sir William Wills. In the following year, four more tobacco companies, and the printers Mardon Son and Hall, all joined Imperial Tobacco.

Duke began his offensive by slashing prices and giving free gifts. Imperial replied with a bonus scheme giving retailers a share of its profits. Duke retaliated by offering to share amongst those traders who would sign an agreement, the whole of Ogdens net profits plus £200,000 a year, for four years. Imperial had the advantage of patriotic support which it exploited by mounting an extensive 'Buy British' campaign. At the same time it was decided to take the war into the enemy's camp by buying an American factory and competing in the USA. Faced with the prospect of tough British com-

OGDENS
GUINEA GOLD 1894-1908
An open-ended series, the biggest ever issued.
Over 8000 different black & white photographs were printed.

petition in his home market and suffering from heavy financial losses in the UK, Duke called for peace talks. On 26 September 1902, Ogdens was sold to Imperial for fifteen million dollars, although a part of this sum was subsequently paid to tobacconists as compensation for breach of the Ogden's contract. The American Tobacco Company also undertook to stop trading in Great Britain and Ireland, whilst Imperial agreed not to enter the American market. It was mutually decided that the export business of both sides would be handled by an entirely new company, British American Tobacco. Duke's final defeat came in 1911 when the US Government secured a declaration under the antitrust laws that the American Tobacco Company was a monopoly and an order was made for it to be broken up.

Of course, the tobacco habit was not restricted to Britain and the United States. It was worldwide, with local demand being met either by local manufacturers or by imports from other countries. In the Far East, Murai Bros. in Japan supplied a teeming market which extended into China, and this company began issuing cards in the 1890s, as did the American Cigarette Company in Shanghai. In Australia, the American Tobacco Company of Victoria and its New South Wales counterpart also issued cards before the turn of the century. All four companies were owned by Duke's American Tobacco Company. In South Africa, the Acme Cigarette Company distributed Wills' cards over-stamped with their own name. In South America a multiplicity of small firms were producing their own Spanish and Portuguese language issues, and local companies were circulating their own cards in

ROYAL POSTILLION.

KNIGHT IN ARMOUR.

THE LLANERO. (VENEZUELA.)

THE COSSACK.

Canada, Cuba, India, Malta and Mexico. The European mainland did not follow until much later.

The new century

In the early 1900s, the Imperial Tobacco Company (ITC) had already established itself as the largest UK company and other firms joined, or were taken over, during ensuing decades. Each of the firms which made up ITC however, retained its identity and issued its own series of cigarette cards. Abroad, the British American Tobacco Company (BAT) often circulated the same series but with different backs; for example, a set of 50 Riders of the World, first issued by Players in Britain in 1905, appeared over the next twenty years in various countries with a variety of backs including Wills and Ogdens. Despite the dominance of ITC in the home market, there were at this period something like 150 other companies, usually very small, which were issuing cards in Britain. Their purpose of course was to attract custom and, as most smokers were men, the great majority of series were prepared with that in mind. Pictures of girls were particularly popular. Whether they were called actresses, beauties, star girls, flag girls, sporting girls, music hall artistes, tobacco girls or our girls, was immaterial, so long as they were pretty. The naval and military theme was also prominent, with pictures of soldiers, and sailors, their uniforms, medals and badges, armaments and vessels, and portraits of heroes, admirals and generals; most were British or Colonial as was befitting an era when Britain's Empire and military strength were at their peak. The Boer War was the stimulus for many contemporary issues. When it was over, companies turned to

PLAYERS
RIDERS OF THE WORLD 1905 B
SET OF 50
Issued world-wide by various manufacturers.

9

earlier battles for inspiration, with Players producing Life Aboard a Man of War in 1805 and 1905 and Wills their Nelson Series to celebrate the centenary of Trafalgar. Other firms got good mileage from the Russo-Japanese conflict. After women and war, the other great male interest was sport. Cricket and football (both association and rugby) were safe bets to have wide appeal while horse-racing, boxing, cycling and golf were also well represented on cards. Other series in that category concentrated on sports generally, and on sporting events, champions, records, and trophies. Royalty played a big part in world affairs at that time, and Queen Victoria's death in 1901 left the nation in a state of grief that is difficult to imagine today. It led to a spate of issues about the Kings and Queens of England, the royal family and the crowned heads of Europe.

Whilst these themes had a strong influence during the years leading up to the Great War, they were by no means the only topics to be covered. A quick glance through a catalogue of the series from that period reveals an enormous range of titles on art, literature, architecture, views, sayings and proverbs, boy scouts, costumes, flags, animals, fish, birds, butterflies, plants, ships, aviation, general knowledge, personalities, heraldry, smoking, inventions, porcelain, the post, motor cars, the circus, telegraphy, the stage, money, industry, the universe, world records, agriculture, history, geography, Egyptology, occupations, natives, the sea, the police, explorers, and so on. The cards came in all sorts of shapes and sizes using all manner of printing techniques. The subject matter had been carefully researched and descriptive

text on the backs of cards had become standard. As a result, the cards from this era provide a valuable legacy of the life and times, a pool of information which can be, and indeed often is, drawn on today by broadcasting companies, publishers and historians.

The Great War
The outbreak of World War 1 led to a flurry of activity among the tobacco companies. There was a dual motivation. To help the War effort, as was the duty of everyone (and to be seen to be doing so by the Authorities in case of a paper shortage) and to cash in on public interest and curiosity. Portraits of war leaders and generals, scenes from the war, pictures of uniforms, weapons, equipment, and naval vessels there were aplenty. War maps, war trophies, army drill, and flags of the Allies abounded. Later came the VC heroes, with details of their glorious exploits, including a mammoth issue of 200 by Gallahers in 1915 and 1916. All had a propaganda value, emphasising the honour and bravery of the Allies in general and Britons in particular, whilst casting the enemy in the role of cowards and barbarians. There were several unusual series. Early in the War, Wills reproduced on cards twelve of the posters published by the Parliamentary Recruiting Committee and designed to aid the call to arms by a brazen appeal to patriotism. Carreras adopted a different approach with their Raemaekers War Cartoons satirising German treachery and brutality, while Hill's series of cartoons Fragments from France were in a lighter vein. Wills had a more subtle psychology when they issued three series on the architectural treasures of Allied countries occupied or threatened by the Teutonic hordes,

BLACK CAT CIGARETTES

MISUNDERSTOOD

BLACK CAT CIGARETTES

A FACT

BLACK CAT CIGARETTES

THE WIDOWS OF BELGIUM

BLACK CAT CIGARETTES

THE PRISONERS

CARRERAS
RAEMAEKERS WAR CARTOONS 1916 D
SET OF 140
The Germans set a price on the artist's head
as a result of these telling drawings.

their Gems of Belgian, Russian and French architecture. Carreras showed how the Home Front was being held by producing their series of Women on War Work.

The wide circulation of cigarette cards and their reputation for detail and accuracy made them subject to censorship and those series with an overtly military theme, such as Wills' Allied Army Leaders and the same firm's Military Motors actually bore the words 'Passed by Censor' or 'Passed for Publication by the Press Bureau' to allay any fears the public may have had about their falling into the wrong hands. Whether or not the Authorities were directly involved with making 'war casualties' of certain series is not clear, but the fact remains that a series prepared by Wills to commemorate the centenary of Wellington's defeat of the French forces at Waterloo was never actually issued, although a handful of sets escaped the furnace and are keenly sought after today. Not quite so drastic was the fate of Wills' second series of Musical Celebrities which contained eight German artistes. Anti-Prussian feeling was running at such a pitch in 1916 that it was thought wise to withdraw the eight cards concerned and pictures of artistes from other countries were issued in their places.

With the German blockade's increasing toll on the volume of imports reaching Britain's shores, shortage of materials meant that the population had to forego all but the bare essentials with the result that printing of cigarette cards ceased in 1917 not to begin again in any volume until 1922. During the interim, one of the most celebrated of card-issuing

firms ceased trading. This was James Taddy & Co., a company founded in 1750, whose main brand had been 'Myrtle Grove' named after Sir Walter Raleigh's Irish home at Youghal, near Cork, a feature which had been exploited in the company's early advertising: 'At Myrtle Grove Sir Walter Raleigh was soothing his mind with the tobacco he had brought from Virginia when his Irish servant, thinking his master was afire, dashed water over him'.

In 1920, cigarette machine operatives went on strike and, although Taddy's employees were not in the Union, they withdrew their labour. The firm's owner claimed that his workforce was already paid more highly and enjoyed better conditions than the Union was demanding. Accordingly he issued an ultimatum that he would close down the business unless there was an immediate return to work. The strikers stayed out, and in June 1920 he closed down, burning all the labels and refusing to part with the goodwill.

Taddy's left a legacy which has given the firm a measure of immortality – their cards. The first of these came out in 1887 and more than forty different series were produced during the next thirty years. The cards are noted for their high standard, but have not survived in any great quantity and these two factors, together with the spectacular abruptness of the firm's closure, have led to certain of their series becoming exceptionally desirable rarities. As far back as 1976 a set of their Clowns and Circus Artistes, a series of only twenty cards, fetched more than £2,000 at auction.

Between the Wars:
The Golden Age of Cigarette Cards

At the resumption of card-issuing on a large scale in 1922, some firms, for example, Players, with their Cries of London, Miniatures and Players Past and Present, contented themselves with re-issuing some of their pre-War series, but Gallahers produced a fine new set of British Birds, and Churchman underlined their East Anglian ties with two series on Rivers and Broads. Such historical, wildlife, and tranquil-view themes were not accidental. They reflected a tiredness of war, and there was a marked absence, albeit temporary, of military subjects.

During the twenties and thirties the ornate style of pre-Great War printing, and the sometimes rather stilted descriptive language both gave way to a functional mode. The number of tobacco companies continued to decline as the smaller ones went out of business or were taken over by the giants. The bigger firms like Wills and Players built up substantial departments devoted to the production of new series at regular intervals. Some idea of the organisation involved in producing cards, and the size of the audience which they reached, can be gauged from the fact that in the United Kingdom alone well over two thousand different series were issued by about eighty different firms during the period from 1920 to 1940, and in some cases the print-run for an individual series was counted in hundreds of millions – Wills printed 600 million cards for their 1936 issue of Railway Engines. Whilst a great many were thrown away, a considerable proportion was saved by collectors or passed on to children who had devised a number of games involving cigarette cards. A ploy adopted

OGDEN'S CIGARETTES

OGDEN'S CIGARETTES

EFFECTS STUDIO—RAIN EFFECT

BROADCASTING AN OPERETTA FROM THE CONCERT HALL

OGDEN'S CIGARETTES

GRAMOPHONE EFFECTS STUDIO

OGDEN'S CIGARETTES

CONTROL ROOM.
MAINTENANCE ENGINEERS AT WORK

by some firms to encourage collecting a particular series was the production of special albums, which could be purchased for a few pennies from local tobacconists. Wills and Players did this on a big scale, coating the backs of the cards concerned with adhesive so that collectors could 'lick 'n stick'. Of course, with a series of cards being packed in a brand for only a limited period, collecting a complete set was often rather difficult. Some numbers were elusive and others were too plentiful, so that a collector would find himself with only a part set and in need of a source from which to obtain the missing numbers. Other collectors would find that a series of cards which interested them had been issued in a brand they did not like, and indeed there were some collectors who did not smoke at all. Here then was a ready-made market for an organisation which was prepared to acquire, store and sell cards as either odds or complete sets. Such a company was founded in 1927, and became the London Cigarette Card Company Ltd.

Under the leadership of Colonel C.L. Bagnall, the London Cigarette Card Company built up stocks of cards, produced catalogues where none had existed before, and in 1933 founded a magazine for collectors 'Cigarette Card News' which has been published continuously since then. This firm is the equivalent in cartophily (card collecting) to Stanley Gibbons in the field of philately (stamps). Being predominently a mail-order business and having outgrown its headquarters which had been located in London for fifty years, the company moved in 1977 to new premises in the West Country, and is now to be found at Somerton in Somerset. There, in its temperature and humidity controlled stockrooms are many thousands of millions of cards from all corners of the globe. The annual catalogues now come in three volumes which, together with the associated handbooks and guidebooks, form the most comprehensive reference sources available. It also produces special loose-leaf binders in which almost every size of card can be displayed, publishes its monthly magazine for distribution to readers all over the world, and has a special department which arranges auctions held regularly at Caxton Hall in London.

The 1920s and 30s were decades of change. Emancipation meant that women were now a significant proportion of the smoking market and the dominance of male chauvinist series picturing the female form was at an end. Dogs, cats, puppies, pets, birds, butterflies, and flowers filled the gap. There was even a series called 'Prizes for Needlework' from one brave manufacturer. The cinema, and later broadcasting, took over from the music hall as the most popular media for mass entertainment. Motor cars and aeroplanes were everyday objects rather than curious contraptions. In sport, tennis, greyhounds and motor racing were attracting the crowds. Edward had come and gone and George VI was on the throne. And the war clouds were gathering. All these trends can be followed in detail on the cards that were issued during the period.

Some of the changes were dramatic. The development of motor cars between Lambert & Butler's first series on this subject in 1908 and their last in 1934 was quite startling. The contrast between Wills' Aviation (1910) and Player's Aeroplanes (1935) or Aircraft of the RAF (1938) is incredible. Equally marked is the comparison between Lambert & Butler's embryo Wireless Telegraphy set issued in 1909 and Ogdens Broadcasting produced in 1935 by which time the BBC had become a massive undertaking with a staff of thousands. Stars of the silent screen so popular in the 20s issues were almost totally absent from the new era of film series produced in the 30s. These were the days of the big dance bands and Ogdens included a picture of Henry Hall at work with the BBC Dance Orchestra in the Broadcasting series, but it was Lambert & Butler who took the honours for devoting an entire series to Danceband Leaders. Great events were commemorated. Hills were quick to circulate their Crystal Palace Souvenir cards within weeks of the pavilion's destruction in July 1936. George V's Silver Jubilee in 1935 was marked by several issues, as was George VI's coronation. Wills prepared a series on the Life of Edward VIII but the monarch abdicated before the cards could be circulated, and they were destroyed.

The whole essence of the 30s is summed up in Mitchell's Wonderful Century series issued in 1937, which illustrates the latest developments and contrasts them with their equivalent in 1837. One other series by this manufacturer produced around the same time deserves particular mention, the World of Tomorrow. It is an imaginative portrayal of how the future was viewed during that period – splitting the atom, television, robots, space-travel, even hang-gliding, are all prophesied – some accurately, others wildly inaccurately.

World War II

As the decade was drawing to a close, the signs of approaching war were plainly to be seen on the cards. Mention has already been made that continental Europe was largely an area in which cigarette cards were not issued. This was principally because most of these countries had a Tobacco Monopoly under which cards had no competitive promotional value. Nonetheless, German manufacturers were prolific in their issues during the 30s. Encouraged by the Third Reich, their cards often had a sinister purpose: propaganda. Such series emphasised the superiority of the Master Race or Germany's military might, with titles like 'The Fight for the Third Reich' and 'Robber State – England'. Hitler, the Nazi Party, and the Hitler Youth Movement featured prominently, and there were series devoted to the German army on manoeuvres, the launching of new warships, and similar topics. All the ominous signs of the build up towards war were there for all to see early in the decade.

In Britain, the impending war began to have an influence on cards much later, and then mainly in a subtle, instructing, informational, acclimatising sense. In 1937, Churchman showed us the The Navy at Work, Carreras gave us Our Navy, and Jackson produced Life in the Navy. Lambert & Butler's Aeroplane Markings and Player's RAF Badges were also from that year. The pace quickened in 1938. The importance being attached to the urgency of preparing the civilian population to cope with aerial warfare is reflected by the fact that the same semi-official Air Raid Precautions series was distributed by Churchman, Hignett, Mitchell, Ogdens and Wills. In the same year, Ardath issued Life in the Services and National Fitness, Churchman The RAF at Work, Player Aircraft of the RAF and Military Uniforms of the British Empire Overseas, and Teofani weighed in with The Army. In the months leading up to the outbreak of war and immediately after, Lambert & Butler came out with a series on the customs and traditions of the services, Player's circulated their Modern Naval Craft and Uniforms of the Territorial Army and Wills their Life in the RN. In 1940, as in 1917, no more paper could be spared and cards ceased being issued for the duration and some time beyond.

The Post-War Period

The first tobacco company to begin producing pictures after the War was Carreras in 1947. Like most things, paper was still in short supply, and this firm hit upon the idea of printing the pictures on the sliding part of the cigarette carton for collectors to cut out, a process which they continued for a decade producing a total of sixteen different blue and white series. A small firm, Philip Allman, brought out a few series in the 50s, and George Dobie circulated some in the 60s. In 1976 Carreras launched their Black Cat brand and since then have issued seven excellent series which are true successors to pre-war cards. More recently, Players have started issuing cards with their Doncella and Grandee cigars. Whether cigarette cards will again rise to the heights they achieved before the War only time will tell.

But the sparsity of post-war tobacco issues has been compensated in another closely related field, that of trade cards. Trade cards are those which are issued with any product other than tobacco, and today there are literally hundreds of different series introduced every year with such commodities as tea, magazines, cereals, sweets, tyres, beer, petrol, bread, frozen foods, soft drinks, tinned goods, meat extract, newspapers, soap, ice cream and crisps. The origins and development of trade cards are closely allied to their tobacco counterparts. Legendary among such card issuers is the Liebig Company which started distributing them with its meat extract in various European countries around 1880 and has continued to do so right up to the present day, having produced something like two thousand different series in the interim. In the early 1900s the two chocolate manufacturers Cadbury and Fry and the shop chains Home and Colonial and Maypole were among the big names to issue cards. They were joined in the 20s and 30s by the Co-op, Goddard's polish, Guinness, Jacobs biscuits, Knights soap, J. Lyons, MacFisheries, Mars, Maynards, Oxo, Pascall, Sainsburys, Spratts dog food and Typhoo tea, as well as shoals of lesser-known enterprises. However, it is in the post-war period that trade issues have reached their peak. So many companies have recognised the value of cards as an instrument to promote sales – such household names as ABC Cinemas, Bassetts sweets, Trex, Blue Band, Birds Eye foods, Brooke Bond, Burtons biscuits, Castrol oil, the Electricity Board, Chivers jam, Coca-Cola, the Daily Mirror, Diners Club, Elkes biscuits, Findus, Fine Fare, Heinz, Horniman's tea, Kellogg's, Kraft, Lever Brothers, Lipton, Lyons Maid, Mobil, Nabisco, Ovaltine, Polydor records, Quaker Oats, Raleigh bicycles, Regent petroleum, Rowntree Mackintosh, Sellotape, Sharps toffee, The Sun, Twinings tea, Walls, Weetabix and Whitbread. The subjects they have covered are as rich and varied as those which originated from the tobacco companies in an earlier era. This of course adds to the wealth of material available to collectors and accounts for the continued interest in cartophily as a hobby throughout the world.

TADDY ▷
CLOWNS & CIRCUS ARTISTES 1920 E
SET OF 20
This set became the most valuable ever when £2000 was paid for it at auction in 1975. Taddy closed down while they were in preparation so they were not issued. About 15 sets exist today. The backs of the cards are blank and they appear to have been cut by hand.

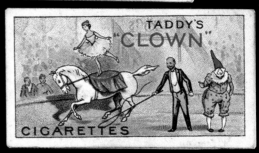

Natural History

Natural History is the most versatile subject covered by the issuers of cigarette cards. All living things the world over – mammals, birds, fish, insects, other creatures, and plants – have been portrayed in hundreds of different series dealing with many facets of this vast subject. Some of the series have been devoted to broad topics like animals or birds, others have concentrated on particular aspects like pond life or parrots. As evolution is a slow process few startling changes can be expected in the subject during the hundred years or so that cards have been produced. Thus the special historical interest so evident in sets illustrating man and his achievements is absent in natural history series. A tiger or a sparrow looks much the same today as it did in the 1890s. Nevertheless, the method of presentation, the emphasis placed on certain subjects, the nature of the descriptive text and even the series title, do reflect a changing outlook on the world about us. Perhaps the most important element here has been the changes in attitudes towards wild life and the role it plays in our environment.

Early series depicting animals tended to dwell on their ferocity (Players Wild Animals 1902), their usefulness to man as sources of fur or ivory (Gallaher Animals and Birds of Commercial Value), or their ability to give pleasure when hunted (Taddy Sports and Pastimes). Similarly with birds; collecting their eggs was a popular pastime and many series were produced to aid identification such as Ogdens Birds Eggs in 1908. Today, wildlife is less plentiful, forests and savannahs have been cultivated and swamps reclaimed. Even in Britain the disappearance of hedgerows in the interests of large-scale farming has destroyed many natural habitats. The widespread use of chemicals has also had its unfortunate side effects on wildlife. The result is that many animals, birds and plants which were commonplace only a few decades ago are now endangered species, and we have become aware of the fact that much of the world's natural heritage is endangered. The collecting of eggs is frowned upon and extraordinary lengths are gone to in order to protect the breeding sites of rare birds. Unregulated hunting is considered now to be an unacceptable pastime so game reserves have been established and laws framed to protect wildlife. Wild fur coats are regarded as being anti-social and wild flowers are for us to enjoy in the countryside, not for picking. These attitudes have become very apparent in current trade series, which have adopted a vanishing wildlife theme, backed by a conservationist stance in their text.

International subjects were prominent in the many sets issued on natural history. British American Tobacco were responsible for some beautiful series from the antipodes. The silk-fronted 'Australian Wild Flowers' is a good example here along with 'Fish of Australia' and 'New Zealand Birds'.

In the 'Golden Age' of cigarette cards between the wars, natural history was, perhaps, the most prolific source of cards when compared with other themes. Flowers, both wild and cultivated, are plentiful although there were not many issues on trees and shrubs. The whole spectrum of the animal world was covered with special emphasis given to cats, dogs, horses and household pets. Dorothy Bagnall notes in her book 'Collecting Cigarette Cards' the originality of treatment of the manufacturers where 'Churchman's "Nature's Architects", Ogden's "Colour in Nature" and Player's "Curious Beaks" are particularly interesting. For quality of production one has only to record the names of Roland Green, who designed "Game Birds and Wild Fowl", and Peter Scott whose pictures were used for the same Company's "Wild Fowl", to illustrate the calibre of the experts who were behind the production of cigarette cards at this time.'

Another interesting trend which can be noticed in natural history cards, apart from the developments in printing techniques and degree of ornamentation, is the fashion in certain subjects. Butterflies and exotic animals for instance, seemed to hold a fascination for Victorian and Edwardian households, Players Butterflies and Moths in 1904 is an attractive example. Fowls and pigeons were also popular, Ogdens Fowls, Pigeons and Dogs in 1904 is an example, if such domesticated birds have a legitimate place in the natural history slot. Between the wars, a greater element of insularity was apparent, with British birds and British animals dominating the scene, sometimes under endearingly sentimental titles like 'Feathered Friends' or 'Little Friends'. In the post-war period, apart from a vogue in pre-historic animals, the main-stream of wildlife series has carried the conservationist torch, whether directly with the 'Vanishing Wildlife', 'North American Wildlife in Danger' approach (Brooke Bond), or more subtly, by emphasizing the beautiful and unusual aspects of nature.

Because of their timelessness, natural history cards have endured the changing fortunes of the last century. Whatever the retail value of these sets, they hold a special place in the hearts of most collectors.

BRITISH BIRDS' EGGS (39) **OGDEN'S CIGARETTES.**
OYSTER-CATCHER.

BRITISH BIRDS' EGGS (40) **OGDEN'S CIGARETTES.**
CORNCRAKE.

BRITISH BIRDS' EGGS (36) **OGDEN'S CIGARETTES.**
CORMORANT.

BRITISH BIRDS' EGGS (37) **OGDEN'S CIGARETTES.**
RAVEN.

BRITISH BIRDS' EGGS (43) **OGDEN'S CIGARETTES.**
GOLDEN EAGLE.

BRITISH BIRDS' EGGS (35) **OGDEN'S CIGARETTES.**
GUILLEMOT.

BRITISH BIRDS' EGGS (38) **OGDEN'S CIGARETTES.**
GREAT AUK.

BRITISH BIRDS' EGGS (48) **OGDEN'S CIGARETTES.**
RAZORBILL.

BRITISH BIRDS' EGGS (33) **OGDEN'S CIGARETTES.**
CURLEW.

BRITISH BIRDS' EGGS (47) **OGDEN'S CIGARETTES.**
WHITETHROAT.

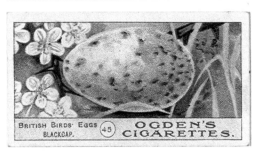

BRITISH BIRDS' EGGS (45) **OGDEN'S CIGARETTES.**
BLACKCAP.

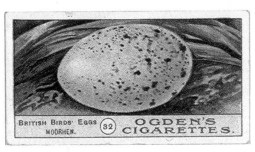

BRITISH BIRDS' EGGS (32) **OGDEN'S CIGARETTES.**
MOORHEN.

BRITISH BIRDS' EGGS (46) **OGDEN'S CIGARETTES.**
COMMON TERN.

BRITISH BIRDS' EGGS (42) **OGDEN'S CIGARETTES.**
COMMON SANDPIPER.

BRITISH BIRDS' EGGS (34) **OGDEN'S CIGARETTES.**
LAPWING.

BRITISH BIRDS' EGGS (41) **OGDEN'S CIGARETTES.**
RING-OUZEL.

BRITISH BIRDS' EGGS (31) **OGDEN'S CIGARETTES.**
RED-BACKED SHRIKE.

BRITISH BIRDS' EGGS (44) **OGDEN'S CIGARETTES.**
STONECHAT.

WILLS'S CIGARETTES.

COREOPSIS.

WILLS'S CIGARETTES.

HELIOTROPIUM.

WILLS'S CIGARETTES.

WALLFLOWERS.

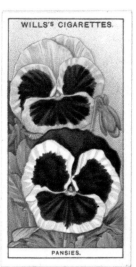

WILLS'S CIGARETTES.

PANSIES.

WILLS'S CIGARETTES.

HELENIUMS.

WILLS'S CIGARETTES.

ALLWOODII.

WILLS'S CIGARETTES.

CARNATION.

WILLS'S CIGARETTES.

PETUNIAS.

WILLS'S CIGARETTES.

ESCHSCHOLTZIAS.

WILLS'S CIGARETTES.

ANTIRRHINUMS.

WILLS'S CIGARETTES.

LUPINES.

WILLS'S CIGARETTES.

VIOLETS.

WILLS'S CIGARETTES.

PYRETHRUMS.

WILLS'S CIGARETTES.

SCABIOUS.

WILLS'S CIGARETTES.

AQUILEGIAS.

WILLS'S CIGARETTES.

CHINESE PINK.

WILLS'S CIGARETTES.

CALENDULA.

WILLS'S CIGARETTES.

LILIUM LONGIFLORUM.

GEUMS.

DAFFODIL.

SNOWDROP.

BEGONIA.

ASTERS.

CHRYSANTHEMUMS.

SWEET PEA.

SUNBEAM POPPIES.

GERANIUM.

VIOLA.

DAHLIA.

NIGELLAS.

VERBENA.

AURICULAS.

PÆONIES.

ANEMONES.

GAILLARDIA.

ZINNIAS.

WILL'S CIGARETTES.

PURPLE LOOSESTRIFE.

WILL'S CIGARETTES.

PRIMROSE.

WILL'S CIGARETTES.

MEADOW CRANE'S-BILL.

WILL'S CIGARETTES.

DWARF FURZE.

WILL'S CIGARETTES.

MARSH MARIGOLD.

WILL'S CIGARETTES.

MARSH MALLOW.

WILL'S CIGARETTES.

FRITILLARY.

WILL'S CIGARETTES.

SUMMER SNOWFLAKE.

WILL'S CIGARETTES.

SUCCORY.

WILL'S CIGARETTES.

COMMON POPPY.

WILL'S CIGARETTES.

TRAVELLER'S JOY.

WILL'S CIGARETTES.

YARROW.

WILL'S CIGARETTES.

DEADLY NIGHTSHADE.

WILL'S CIGARETTES.

CARLINE THISTLE.

WILL'S CIGARETTES.

GREATER KNAPWEED.

WILL'S CIGARETTES.

COMMON ROCK-ROSE.

WILL'S CIGARETTES.

RED CAMPION.

WILL'S CIGARETTES.

SCENTLESS MAY WEED.

WILLS
WILD FLOWERS 1923 A
SET OF 50

WILLS ▷
GARDENING HINTS 1923 A
SET OF 50

WILLS'S CIGARETTES.

FRENCH. PLANTING ASPARAGUS.

WILLS'S CIGARETTES.

SOWING PEAS.

WILLS'S CIGARETTES.

MAKING A LAWN.

WILLS'S CIGARETTES.

STAKING CHRYSANTHEMUMS.

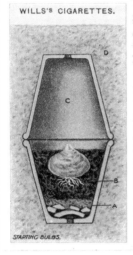

WILLS'S CIGARETTES.

STARTING BULBS.

WILLS'S CIGARETTES.

STAKING.

WILLS'S CIGARETTES.

RINGING.

WILLS'S CIGARETTES.

STEM-LAYERING.

WILLS'S CIGARETTES.

RE-POTTING.

WILLS'S CIGARETTES.

EARWIG TRAP.

WILLS'S CIGARETTES.

SUMMER PRUNING OF ROSES.

WILLS'S CIGARETTES.

ROOTING SHRUB CUTTINGS.

WILLS'S CIGARETTES.

IN-ARCHING.

WILLS'S CIGARETTES.

HOME-MADE PROPAGATING FRAME.

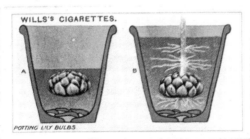

WILLS'S CIGARETTES.

POTTING LILY BULBS.

WILLS'S CIGARETTES.

PLANTING TREES.

WILLS'S CIGARETTES.

DIVIDING BEGONIAS.

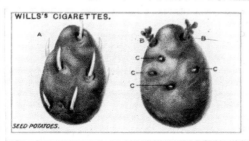

WILLS'S CIGARETTES.

SEED POTATOES.

WILLS'S CIGARETTES.

SIMPLE PROPAGATORS.

EDWARDS RINGER & BIGG
DOGS 1908 B
SET OF 23

PLAYER'S CIGARETTES — SHORT-HAIRED BLACK

PLAYER'S CIGARETTES — SHORT-HAIRED BLACK AND WHITE

PLAYER'S CIGARETTES — SHORT-HAIRED BROWN TABBY

PLAYER'S CIGARETTES — SHORT-HAIRED TORTOISESHELL

PLAYER'S CIGARETTES — HAIRED TORTOISESHELL AND WHITE

PLAYER'S CIGARETTES — LONG-HAIRED BROWN TABBY

PLAYER'S CIGARETTES — LONG-HAIRED CREAM

PLAYER'S CIGARETTES — LONG-HAIRED RED TABBY

PLAYER'S CIGARETTES

PLAYER'S CIGARETTES

PLAYER'S CIGARETTES

PLAYER'S CIGARETTES

LE OPARD

HIPP OPOTA MUS

IGUANA

ANT ELO PE

BUF FA LO

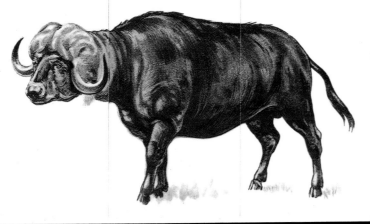

WAP IT M

"ANIMALLOYS"

AN UN-NATURAL HISTORY SERIES

48 SUBJECTS — NUMBER 38

This card shows a section of a well-known animal, the sections needed to complete the animal appearing on two other cards. The complete series comprises 16 animals, each in three sections, and by mixing the sections you can produce a large number of strange creatures with amusing names.

W. D. & H. O. WILLS

ISSUED BY THE IMPERIAL TOBACCO CO. (OF GREAT BRITAIN & IRELAND), LIMITED.

SMALL TORTOISESHELL.

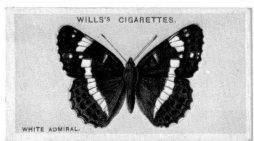
WHITE ADMIRAL.

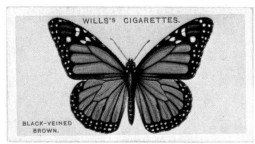
BLACK-VEINED BROWN.

SMALL COPPER.

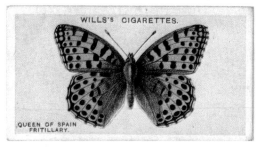
QUEEN OF SPAIN FRITILLARY.

BROWN HAIRSTREAK.

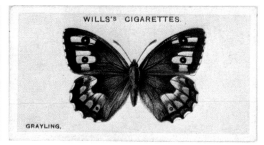
GRAYLING.

PAINTED LADY.

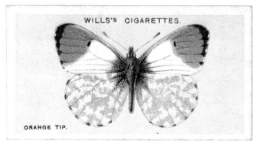
ORANGE TIP.

PURPLE HAIRSTREAK.

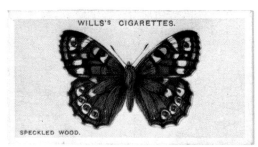
SPECKLED WOOD.

SWALLOW-TAIL.

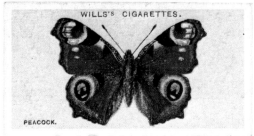
PEACOCK.

MARBLED WHITE.

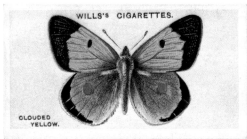
CLOUDED YELLOW.

BATH WHITE.

WILLS
BRITISH BUTTERFLIES 1927 B
SET OF 50

Player's Cigarettes	*Player's Cigarettes*	*Player's Cigarettes*	*Player's Cigarettes*	*Player's Cigarettes*	*Player's Cigarettes*
Red-Collared Lorikeet	Rosy-Faced Love-Bird	Nonpareil Bunting	Nonpareil (Pintailed) Grass Finch	Greenfinch-Bullfinch Hybrid	Black-Headed Gouldian Finch
Player's Cigarettes	*Player's Cigarettes*	*Player's Cigarettes*	*Player's Cigarettes*	*Player's Cigarettes*	*Player's Cigarettes*
Red-Headed Gouldian Finch	Superb Tanager	Australian Crimson Finch	Goldfinch-Canary Mule	Bullfinch-Canary Mule	Black-Headed Siskin
Player's Cigarettes	*Player's Cigarettes*	*Player's Cigarettes*	*Player's Cigarettes*	*Player's Cigarettes*	*Player's Cigarettes*
Lizard Canary	Virginian Cardinal	Napoleon Weaver-Bird	Goldfinch-Bullfinch Hybrid	Blue-Fronted Amazon Parrot	Yellow Cinnamon Canary

PLAYERS
AVIARY & CAGE BIRDS 1933 B
SET OF 50
A set of transfers was also issued in the same year.
(see page 48).

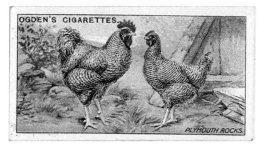

OGDENS
POULTRY 1915 B
SET OF 25
Two sets were issued in the same year.
One with 'Ogdens' on the front, the other without.

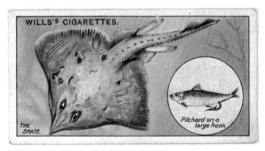

WILLS
FISH AND BAIT 1910 B
SET OF 50

29

Land, Sea and Air

At the time when the first cigarette cards were being issued, the only form of mechanized land transport was the railway, and even that was a comparatively recent innovation. The internal combustion engine had not been invented and steam was supreme. On the seas, sailing power was only just giving way to steam and the aeroplane was a dream of the future. This then was the image portrayed on most Victorian cards.

By the turn of the century, however, some important developments were to be observed. The motor car had arrived, and some of the early models, playthings for the rich fanatic, appear among that immense series of thousands of photographs issued by Ogdens with their Guinea Gold cigarettes from 1894 to 1908. In the latter year, the motor car had established itself sufficiently as a serious mode of transport for Lambert & Butler to devote a whole series to the subject with names which are now so evocative to the veteran enthusiast, Mors, De Dion Bouton and Rolls-Royce. The skies were no longer the exclusive preserve of winged creatures; weird contraptions, aeroplanes, were beginning to establish landmarks in aviation, and Wills, in 1910, were the first of many firms to depict this topic on cards, with a combination of lighter-than-air airships and heavier-than-air aeroplanes.

War has often proved a spur to man's powers of invention and application. Cards issued around the time of the Great War demonstrate the point. Military dirigibles and fighting aircraft are shown in Lambert & Butler's Aviation series (1915-16), the role of the internal combustion engine in war was depicted in Wills Military Motors (1916), and steam-based naval might was typified by the same company's series of The World's Dreadnoughts.

In the 20s the application of mass-production techniques brought down the cost of motor cars within the reach of many families, revolutionized the distribution of goods, and gave omnibus operators the means of providing a cheap and flexible network of mass transport which accelerated the growth of suburbia and served almost every village and hamlet in the land. Whilst air travel was still in a pioneering stage, the seeds of future developments had been sown. The first regular public air services were introduced, mail was carried, and Croydon aerodrome expanded to serve as London's airport. However, the railways remained the most important means of land travel for both passengers and goods. Overseas travel and international trade were almost entirely dependent on shipping.

The 30s saw the continuation of these trends. With the 20s, they were also the great heyday of card issues. Thousands of series of cards on all manner of subjects were produced in the United Kingdom, and thousands more worldwide. Travel and transport were well represented, and they clearly show the rapid changes that were taking place. In the fifteen years between Lambert & Butler's 1922 series of Motor Cars and the Player issue of 1937, vehicles had altered almost beyond recognition. Many of the old railway companies were amalgamated, electrification on the Southern Region extended commuter territory to the coast. A great network of deep tube constructions criss-crossed London, huge new transatlantic liners were launched, and air travel became commonplace. Speed had become an obsession, with one record after another being smashed.

When Wills issued their second set of Speed in 1938, they included the latest record-holders, 357 mph on land, 440 mph in the air, 130 mph on water. In their first series of Speed produced eight years previously, the records stood at 231 mph, 357 mph and 93 mph respectively. Both these series show a selection of aircraft, cars, cycles, trains and ships which were the marvel of their day. Names which bring memories flooding back for many people alive today: Spitfire, Thunderbolt, Bluebird, The Coronation Scot, The Queen Mary. Entire series were devoted to specific aspects of transport – Life in a Liner, The Queen Mary, The Blue Riband of the Atlantic, Construction of Railway Trains, Railway Equipment, Wonderful Railway Travel, A Day on the Airway, International Airliners, Empire Air Routes, Hints and Tips for Motorists, How Motor Cars Work, Motor Index Marks, each giving a fascinatingly different insight into the world as it was in those days leading up to the war.

With such a wealth of material to choose from, it is easy for the collector to turn back the clock and immerse himself in nostalgia, to wallow in the splendour of the great Atlantic liners, to join Imperial Airways on a flight to Bombay, to lunch in the restaurant car on the Flying Scotsman, to arrive at Gleneagles in a Bugatti. Magic!

Of course, the war changed many things. Few cigarette cards have been issued since, and it has been left to the non-tobacco firms to record on their cards the changes which have taken place in travel and transport – the dominance of the motor and air travel, the decline of the railways and ocean travel, and the dawning of the space age.

LAMBERT & BUTLER'S
CIGARETTES

AUSTIN SEVEN SALOON DE LUXE

LAMBERT & BUTLER'S
CIGARETTES

MORRIS MINOR SALOON

LAMBERT & BUTLER'S
CIGARETTES

JOWETT "KESTREL" SALOON

LAMBERT & BUTLER'S
CIGARETTES

ROVER "TEN" SALOON

LAMBERT & BUTLER'S
CIGARETTES

CROSSLEY TEN
"TORQUAY" SALOON

LAMBERT & BUTLER'S
CIGARETTES

RENAULT 12 H.P. SALOON

LAMBERT & BUTLER'S
CIGARETTES

MORRIS TEN FOUR SALOON

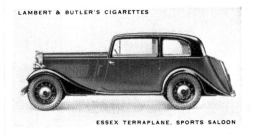

LAMBERT & BUTLER'S CIGARETTES

ESSEX TERRAPLANE, SPORTS SALOON

LAMBERT & BUTLER'S
CIGARETTES

HILLMAN MINX SALOON DE LUXE

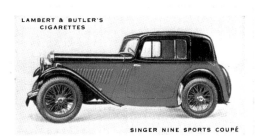

LAMBERT & BUTLER'S
CIGARETTES

SINGER NINE SPORTS COUPÉ

LAMBERT & BUTLER'S
CIGARETTES

HUMBER "TWELVE" SALOON

LAMBERT & BUTLER'S
CIGARETTES

FORD V-8 SALOON DE LUXE

LAMBERT & BUTLER'S
CIGARETTES

STANDARD NINE SALOON

LAMBERT & BUTLER'S
CIGARETTES

FORD 8 H.P. SALOON

LAMBERT & BUTLER'S
CIGARETTES

LANCHESTER "10" SALOON

LAMBERT & BUTLER'S
CIGARETTES

B.S.A. 10 H.P. SALOON

LAMBERT & BUTLER'S
CIGARETTES

WOLSELEY HORNET SALOON

LAMBERT & BUTLER'S CIGARETTES

M.G. MIDGET

LAMBERT & BUTLER'S
CIGARETTES

CITROËN "TEN" SALOON DE LUXE

LAMBERT & BUTLER'S
CIGARETTES

WOLSELEY NINE SALOON

LAMBERT & BUTLER'S CIGARETTES

TRIUMPH "GLORIA" SALOON

PLAYER'S CIGARETTES

AUSTIN FOURTEEN "GOODWOOD" SALOON

PLAYER'S CIGARETTES

AUBURN SUPER-CHARGED SPEEDSTER

PLAYER'S CIGARETTES

BUGATTI TYPE 57. S "COMPETITION" MODEL

PLAYER'S CIGARETTES

BUICK "EMPIRE" SALOON

PLAYER'S CIGARETTES

CITROËN "SPORTS TWELVE" SALOON

PLAYER'S CIGARETTES

LAGONDA 7-SEATER LIMOUSINE

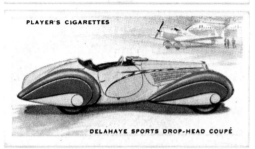

PLAYER'S CIGARETTES

DELAHAYE SPORTS DROP-HEAD COUPÉ

PLAYER'S CIGARETTES

STUDEBAKER DICTATOR DE LUXE SALOON

PLAYER'S CIGARETTES

TALBOT "3½-LITRE" DROP-HEAD FOURSOME COUPÉ

PLAYER'S CIGARETTES

BRITISH SALMSON 14 H.P. SALOON

PLAYER'S CIGARETTES

HILLMAN HAWK SALOON

PLAYER'S CIGARETTES

SINGER 12 H.P. SALOON

PLAYER'S CIGARETTES

LANCHESTER "14" ROADRIDER SPORTS SALOON

PLAYER'S CIGARETTES

"FLYING STANDARD" 20 H.P. V-EIGHT SALOON

PLAYER'S CIGARETTES

LANCIA-APRILIA STANDARD PILLARLESS SALOON

PLAYER'S CIGARETTES

HUDSON EIGHT SALOON DE LUXE

PLAYER'S CIGARETTES

WOLSELEY 25 H.P. SUPER SIX SPORTSMAN'S SALOON

PLAYER'S CIGARETTES

ROVER SIXTEEN SPORTS SALOON

◁ LAMBERT & BUTLER
MOTOR CARS 1934 A
SET OF 25

32

PLAYERS
MOTOR CARS 2ND SERIES 1937 B
SET OF 50
The first series was issued in 1936.
One of many sets with adhesive backs.

PLAYER'S CIGARETTES

SUNBEAM THIRTY SEDANCA DE VILLE

PLAYER'S CIGARETTES

MORRIS FOURTEEN-SIX (SERIES II) SALOON

PLAYER'S CIGARETTES

M.G. MIDGET SERIES "T" TWO-SEATER

PLAYER'S CIGARETTES

PACKARD "120" TOURING COUPÉ

PLAYER'S CIGARETTES

LAMMAS GRAHAM FOURSOME DROP-HEAD COUPÉ

PLAYER'S CIGARETTES

MORGAN "4-4"

PLAYER'S CIGARETTES

S.S. 2½-LITRE JAGUAR "100"

PLAYER'S CIGARETTES

BENTLEY 4-SEATER COUPÉ

PLAYER'S CIGARETTES

ALVIS 4·3-LITRE VANDEN PLAS SALOON

PLAYER'S CIGARETTES

PONTIAC DE LUXE EIGHT SPORTS COUPÉ

PLAYER'S CIGARETTES

LINCOLN-ZEPHYR SALOON

PLAYER'S CIGARETTES

MERCEDES-BENZ TYPE 540 COUPÉ

PLAYER'S CIGARETTES

RAILTON FAIRMILE COUPÉ

PLAYER'S CIGARETTES

A.C. GREYHOUND SALOON

PLAYER'S CIGARETTES

DAIMLER "LIGHT STRAIGHT-EIGHT"

PLAYER'S CIGARETTES

FIAT "500" CONVERTIBLE SALOON

PLAYER'S CIGARETTES

RILEY NINE MONACO SALOON

PLAYER'S CIGARETTES

HUMBER SNIPE SPORTS SALOON

PLAYER'S CIGARETTES

CORD SPORTSMAN'S CONVERTIBLE COUPÉ

PLAYER'S CIGARETTES

SIDDELEY SPECIAL TOURING LIMOUSINE

PLAYER'S CIGARETTES

FRAZER-NASH-B.M.W. TYPE 326/50 SALOON

ARTICULATED HEAVY FREIGHT LOCO., NORTHERN PACIFIC RAILWAY, U.S.A.

EXPRESS LOCOMOTIVE, MADRID, ZARAGOZA & ALICANTE RLY., SPAIN

MIXED-TRAFFIC LOCOMOTIVE, CANTON-HANKOW RAILWAY, CHINA

"PACIFIC" EXPRESS LOCOMOTIVE "PRINCESS MARGARET ROSE," L.M.S.R.

STREAMLINED EXPRESS LOCOMOTIVE "SILVER LINK," L.N.E.R.

ARTICULATED LOCOMOTIVE "EMIR OF KATSINA," NIGERIAN GOVT. RLY.

"SCHOOLS" CLASS LOCOMOTIVE "LEATHERHEAD," SOUTHERN RAILWAY

EXPRESS LOCOMOTIVE "MOHAMED ALI EL KEBIR," EGYPTIAN STATE RLYS.

STREAMLINED LOCO. "COMMODORE VANDERBILT," N.Y.C. RAILROAD, U.S.A.

HEAVY FREIGHT LOCO., BUENOS AYRES & PACIFIC RLY., ARGENTINA

EXPRESS PASSENGER LOCO., NORTHERN PACIFIC RAILWAY, U.S.A.

EXPRESS LOCOMOTIVE, IMPERIAL GOVERNMENT RAILWAYS OF JAPAN

EXPRESS LOCOMOTIVE, NEW ZEALAND GOVERNMENT RAILWAYS

SUBURBAN TANK LOCOMOTIVE, EASTERN RAILWAY, FRANCE

ARTICULATED EXPRESS LOCOMOTIVE, SAN PAULO (BRAZILIAN) RAILWAY

EXPRESS LOCOMOTIVE, CANADIAN NATIONAL RAILWAYS

EXPRESS LOCOMOTIVE "SILVER JUBILEE," L.M.S.R.

PASSENGER & FREIGHT LOCOMOTIVE, KENYA & UGANDA RAILWAYS

WILLS'S CIGARETTES
EXPRESS LOCOMOTIVE, AUSTRIAN FEDERAL RAILWAYS.

WILLS'S CIGARETTES
HEAVY FREIGHT TANK LOCOMOTIVE, NETHERLANDS RAILWAYS.

WILLS'S CIGARETTES
TURBINE-DRIVEN LOCOMOTIVE, L.M.S.R.

WILLS'S CIGARETTES
EXPRESS LOCOMOTIVE "KESTREL," GREAT NORTHERN RLY., IRELAND

WILLS'S CIGARETTES
DIESEL-ELECTRIC TRAIN "BURLINGTON ZEPHYR," C.B. & Q. RAILROAD, U.S.A.

WILLS'S CIGARETTES
HEAVY FREIGHT LOCOMOTIVE, U.S.S.R. RAILWAYS

WILLS'S CIGARETTES
STREAMLINED EXPRESS LOCOMOTIVE, BELGIAN NATIONAL RAILWAYS

WILLS'S CIGARETTES
EXPRESS LOCOMOTIVE "DUKE OF ABERCORN," N.C.C. (L.M.S.R.), IRELAND

WILLS'S CIGARETTES
DRUMM BATTERY TRAIN, GREAT SOUTHERN RAILWAYS, IRELAND

WILLS'S CIGARETTES
"PACIFIC" EXPRESS LOCOMOTIVE "PAPYRUS," L.N.E.R.

WILLS'S CIGARETTES
EXPRESS LOCOMOTIVE, NORTH WESTERN RAILWAY, INDIA

WILLS'S CIGARETTES
EXPRESS LOCOMOTIVE, GERMAN STATE RAILWAYS

WILLS'S CIGARETTES
HEAVY PASSENGER AND FREIGHT LOCOMOTIVE, CANADIAN PACIFIC RLY.

WILLS'S CIGARETTES
2 FT. 6 IN. GAUGE LOCOMOTIVE, LITHUANIAN STATE RAILWAYS

WILLS'S CIGARETTES
ELECTRIC PASSENGER AND FREIGHT LOCOMOTIVE, SWISS FEDERAL RLYS.

WILLS'S CIGARETTES
"CASTLE" CLASS EXPRESS LOCOMOTIVE "WINDSOR CASTLE," G.W.R.

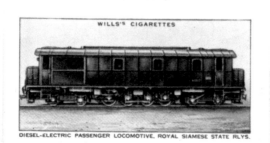
WILLS'S CIGARETTES
DIESEL-ELECTRIC PASSENGER LOCOMOTIVE, ROYAL SIAMESE STATE RLYS.

WILLS'S CIGARETTES
EXPRESS LOCOMOTIVE, BENGAL-NAGPUR RAILWAY, INDIA

HAWKER "HURRICANE" FIGHTER

H.M.S. "THAMES"

"CORONATION SCOT" EXPRESS, L.M.S.R.

THE "NORMANDIE"

H.M. MOTOR TORPEDO-BOAT No. 102

SANTA FE "SUPER CHIEF" DIESEL FLYER

SPEED-BOAT "NOTRE DAME"

"BRISTOLIAN" EXPRESS, G.W.R.

NAPIER RAILTON (JOHN COBB)

THE "QUEEN MARY"

"CORONATION" EXPRESS, L.N.E.R.

SAVOIA-MARCHETTI S-79 BOMBER

"THUNDERBOLT" (CAPTAIN G. E. T. EYSTON)

SHORT "EMPIRE" FLYING-BOAT TRANSPORT

OUTBOARD MOTOR-BOAT "CHICK III"

248 c.c. GUZZI (OMOBONO TENNI)

STREAMLINED PROPELLER RAILCAR

M.G. MAGNETTE (MAJOR A. T. G. GARDNER)

PLAYERS
SPEED 1938 A
SET OF 50

MACCHI-CASTOLDI 72 RACER

"PRINCESS ELIZABETH", L.M.S.R.

"MORMON METEOR" (AB JENKINS)

SUPERMARINE "SPITFIRE" FIGHTER

494 c.c. B.M.W. (J. M. WEST)

H.M.S. "ICARUS"

"SPEED OF THE WIND" (CAPTAIN G. E. T. EYSTON & A. DENLY)

E.R.A. (RAYMOND MAYS)

DE HAVILLAND "COMET" RACER

SIR MALCOLM CAMPBELL'S "BLUEBIRD"

MERCEDES-BENZ (RUDOLF CARACCIOLA)

THE "STIRLING CASTLE"

494 c.c. B.M.W. (ERNST HENNE)

PERCIVAL "MEW GULL" III RACER

GERMAN DIESEL FLYERS

AUTO-UNION (BERND ROSEMEYER)

"DENVER ZEPHYR" DIESEL FLYER

ARMSTRONG-WHITWORTH "ENSIGN" TRANSPORT

A CIRCULAR IRONCLAD.

A STEAM SUBMARINE.

A TRAIN FERRY.

A WHALE-CATCHER.

A MUD HOPPER.

THE "FRESNO."

A FLOATING DOCK.

A MONITOR.

AN EXPERIMENTAL CRAFT.

A BUCKET DREDGER.

H.M.S. "HERMES."

A FLOATING HOTEL.

A GRAB DREDGER.

THE "SPURN."

A MONITOR-TYPE FREIGHTER.

THE "PATOKA."

H.M.S. "RODNEY."

THE "PETER STUYVESANT."

WILLS
STRANGE CRAFT 1931 B
SET OF 50

38

S.S. BELGENLAND.

R.M.S. WINDSOR CASTLE.

S.S. NALDERA.

R.M.S. AQUITANIA.

S.S. DUILIO.

S.S. GIULIO CESARE.

S.S. LAPLAND.

S.S. FRANCE.

R.M.S. LACONIA.

R.M.S. FRANCONIA.

R.M.S. SCYTHIA.

S.S. CELTIC.

S.S. LEVIATHAN.

S.S. MONTLAURIER.

R.M.S. BERENGARIA.

S.S. MAJESTIC.

S.S. NARKUNDA.

S.S. EMPRESS OF FRANCE.

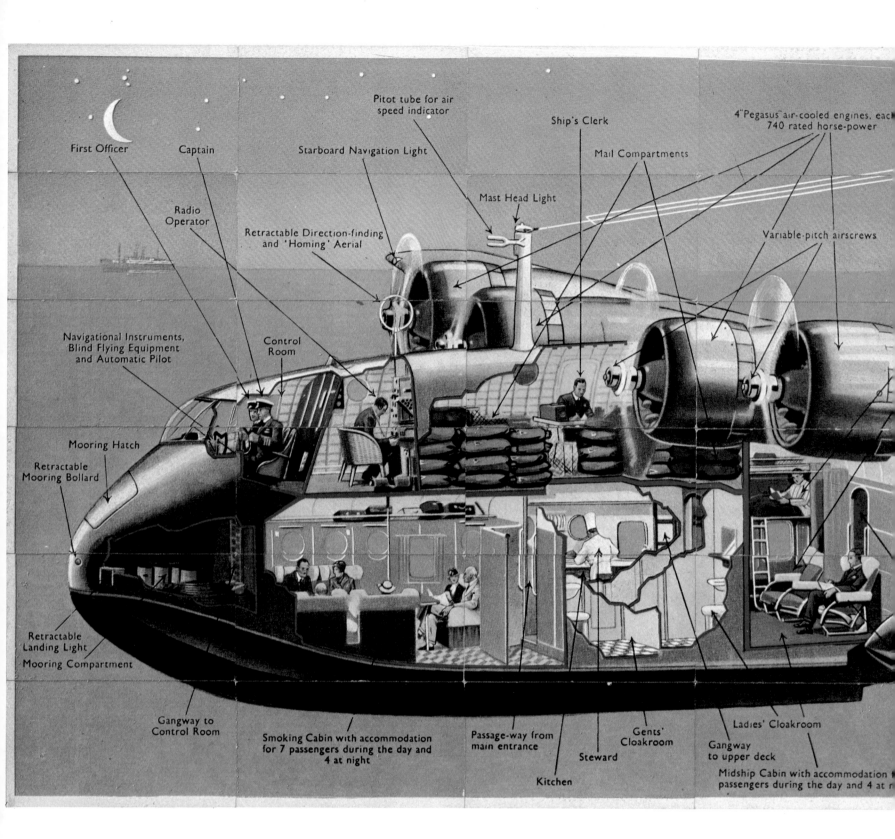

First Officer

Captain

Pitot tube for air
speed indicator

Ship's Clerk

4"Pegasus"air-cooled engines, each
740 rated horse-power

Radio
Operator

Starboard Navigation Light

Mail Compartments

Mast Head Light

Variable-pitch airscrews

Retractable Direction-finding
and 'Homing' Aerial

Navigational Instruments,
Blind Flying Equipment
and Automatic Pilot

Control
Room

Mooring Hatch

Retractable
Mooring Bollard

Retractable
Landing Light

Mooring Compartment

Gangway to
Control Room

Smoking Cabin with accommodation
for 7 passengers during the day and
4 at night

Passage-way from
main entrance

Kitchen

Steward

Gents'
Cloakroom

Ladies' Cloakroom

Gangway
to upper deck

Midship Cabin with accommodation
passengers during the day and 4 at n

ARDATH
EMPIRE FLYING BOAT 1938 B
SET OF 48
An impressive sectional set
reproduced slightly smaller than actual size.

All-metal wing

Fixed aerial

International Registration Marking

...ping berths

Port Navigation Light

Flaps fitted to trailing edges of the wing

Freight Hatch

...d for bedding

Metal Hull

Mail, Freight and Baggage Hold

Promenade Cabin with accommodation for 8 passengers during the day and 4 at night

After Cabin with accommodation for 6 passengers during the day and 4 at night

Main gangway

Wing-tip float

...djustable chairs

PLAYER'S CIGARETTES

C.L.S.: FOKKER F. XVIII

PLAYER'S CIGARETTES

AIR FRANCE: LIORE-ET-OLIVIER H. 24-2

PLAYER'S CIGARETTES

CENTRAL AIRLINES: STINSON "A"

PLAYER'S CIGARETTES

A.B. AEROTRANSPORT: FOKKER F. XII "VÄRMLAND"

PLAYER'S CIGARETTES

SWISSAIR: LOCKHEED "ORION"

PLAYER'S CIGARETTES

IMPERIAL AIRWAYS FLYING-BOAT "SATYRUS"

PLAYER'S CIGARETTES

IMPERIAL AIRWAYS LINER "DRYAD": "DIANA" CLASS

PLAYER'S CIGARETTES

QANTAS EMPIRE AIRWAYS LINER "COMMONWEALTH" CLASS

PLAYER'S CIGARETTES

IMPERIAL AIRWAYS LINER "SCYLLA"

PLAYER'S CIGARETTES

TRANS-CONTINENTAL AND WESTERN AIR: DOUGLAS D.C. 2

PLAYER'S CIGARETTES

IMPERIAL AIRWAYS LINER "HORATIUS": "HERACLES" CLASS

PLAYER'S CIGARETTES

AIR FRANCE: WIBAULT-PENHOËT 282-T-12

PLAYER'S CIGARETTES

DEUTSCHE LUFT HANSA: JUNKERS G. 38

PLAYER'S CIGARETTES

EASTERN AIRLINES: DOUGLAS D.C. 2

PLAYER'S CIGARETTES

AEROPUT: DE HAVILLAND DRAGON-RAPIDE

PLAYER'S CIGARETTES

S.A.B.E.N.A.: FOKKER F. VII. 3M

PLAYER'S CIGARETTES

ALA LITTORIA: CANT Z. 506 SEAPLANE

PLAYER'S CIGARETTES

K.L.M. (ROYAL DUTCH AIRLINES) FOKKER F. XXII

PLAYERS
INTERNATIONAL AIR LINERS 1936   A
SET OF 50

MID-OCEAN AIRPORT

COMPOSITE AIRCRAFT

SUPER-AIRPLANE

BIRDMAN

STREAM-LINED SPEED-SHIP

TELEVISION

LAUNCHING A SPACE-SHIP

STREAM-LINED TRAIN

GYRO-MOTOR RACE

TUNNEL TRAVEL

CATHODE ROCKET SPACE-SHIP

RAILPLANE

INSIDE A SPACE-SHIP

ROAD LINER

ROCKET POST

ONE-MAN SUBMARINE

FOG ELIMINATOR

LONDON OF THE FUTURE

MITCHELL
WORLD OF TOMORROW 1936 A
SET OF 50
Issued in black & white.

Novelties

Most cartophilic items are cigarette cards or trade cards, and, despite variations in size, they conform to a pattern. Yet there is a wealth of material outside the standard issues worthy of comment. Errors and varieties make an interesting group. A classic example of a mistake made by an artist is demonstrated on No 43 of Players Dandies, where Disraeli is depicted as a man of twenty-two with the outline of Big Ben behind him. Unfortunately, the famous clock was not installed until 32 years later. A hurried attempt was made to erase the tower, but its shadow was still discernible. Eventually a replacement card was issued on which the entire background had been removed. Errors have also been made in numbering, factual information, colour printing, and so on. Varieties appear, for example, when the picture or text was revised during a print-run to bring it up-to-date.

There are also many examples of unorthodox series in one form or another. These are known usually as novelties. There are sectional series such as the Famous Pictures produced by Wills in the early 30s where the cards make up into a painting; the Cycling Map put out by Ogdens; and the Coronation Procession of George VI from the same firm. Other companies, such as Godfrey Phillips and Guinness, issued cards with postcard backs which could be mailed whilst some circulated playing cards, or normal cards with a miniature playing card inset in one corner. There are shaped cards designed as lapel badges, push-out cards where the outline of a soldier, a bird, or national costume, was die-cut so that it could be pressed out and made to stand up (Ogdens were fond of this idea), and pull-outs like Godfrey Phillips Novelty Series where the cards were in two parts slotted together and which, when pulled slowly apart, caused the image to change. Sarony produced cards with holes punched in the margin so that they could be inserted in special miniature binders supplied by the company and several firms packed with their cigarettes objects like booklets (e.g. Carreras French-English Dictionary), rules for card games, sports fixture cards, calendars, bookmarks, and Christmas greetings. Another popular departure from the ordinary card was the transfer, whereby the image could be conveyed to another surface when wetted. Players issued several of their 1930s series in this form. Other variations were cards with invisible ink where a picture or writing would appear when the surface was exposed to heat, rubbed with a hard object or had water applied to it.

The stereoscopic card made an appearance in the 20s. Cavanders produced several series, particularly scenes, consisting of a left and a right card for each number which, when looked at through a special viewer, gave a three dimensional effect.

Paper and card, however, were not the only materials from which cartophilic items were made. Silk, satin, canvas, felt, lace, metal and plastic have all been utilized. Amongst these, silk had the widest application. The pictures were either printed or embroidered on the silk, and sometimes a paper-backing was added to give rigidity and a second surface for printing. The most prolific issuers of silks were Godfrey Phillips who produced fifty different unbacked series, often inscribed with their B.D.V. Cigarettes label. Birds, flags, heraldry, military badges and paintings predominated, although they did select some very original subjects such as Irish Patriots. Godfrey Phillips awarded prizes for the best objects made from their silks, receiving cushion covers, counterpanes, and even garments. But probably the best known silks were those from the firm of J. Wix, makers of Kensitas Cigarettes. They produced printed silks of National Flags and British Empire Flags protected by transparent paper, and the delightfully embroidered 'Kensitas Flowers' encapsulated in yellow folders. These were turned out by the million and are easy to collect today.

Canvas, or to be more accurate, linen fabric glazed to give the appearance of canvas, was used by firms like Hill to give an extra touch of authenticity to their reproductions of oil paintings, and some companies, particularly in America, used a felt-like material from which miniature rugs and flags were made. Carreras diverged into fabrics and came up with a new angle, lace motifs.

Metal was used by some manufacturers to bring an element of novelty to their inserts. As early as 1901, Wills issued with their Firefly cigarettes a series of ten mixed brass and bronze medalets, each depicting a member of the Royal Family or a hero of the Boer War with a loop at the top enabling them to be attached to watch chains. In 1914, the same firm's export department brought out a set of elegant oval-shaped miniature portraits of famous women, enamalled in colour on metal and for which a special frame could be obtained free of charge in exchange for 25 coupons. Cohen Weenen went one stage further and issued a series of portraits each of which was ready-housed in an ornate miniature metal frame. In the 30s the International Tobacco Company used thin cold-stamped bronze as the medium for their series of reliefs showing famous British buildings and monuments and Rothmans produced in base metal a series of charms for attaching to a bracelet.

Finally, if honours were awarded for originality in cartophily, the Record Cigarette Company of London would be high on the list. During the 30s they produced a 'Variety Series' of twenty-five 'Talkie' cigarette cards, the reverse of which comprised miniature gramophone records

MINIATURE CARDS

WILLS

BEAUTIES, PLAYING CARD INSET 1897 E

SET OF 52

45

DIE-CUTS, OVALS AND CIRCULARS

KINNEY
NOVELTIES (DIE-CUT) 1888 E
SET OF 75
Issued by a US manufacturer whose cards
and novelties are highly valued today.

BLANKETS AND RUGS

SPLENDID EXAMPLES OF FELTS AND MINIATURE RUGS
FROM THE US. ACTUAL SIZE SHOWN. ▷

ASSORTED NOVELTIES

1 MURATTI
ACTRESSES & BEAUTIES 1899 D (each card)
Set length uncertain

2 CARRERAS
BLACK CAT HANDY FRENCH-ENGLISH
DICTIONARY 1915 A
Single

3 GODFREY PHILLIPS
CINEMA STARS 1924 A
SET OF 25

4 WILLS
AVIARY & CAGE BIRDS (transfers) 1933 B
SET OF 50

5 PLAYERS
ADVERTISEMENT CARD (Sailor) 1929 A
Single
The famous trademark painted by T.H. Fisher

6 RECORD CIGARETTE CO
'TALKIE CARD' 1936 E
SET OF 25
(back of card)

7 LLOYD
STAR GIRLS 1899 E
SET OF 25

8 WILLS
SOLDIERS OF THE WORLD 1895 E
SET OF 100

9 CARRERAS
'ROUND THE WORLD' SCENIC MODELS 1925 B
SET OF 50

10 MAJOR DRAPKIN
SOLDIERS & THEIR UNIFORMS 1914 B
SET OF 25

11 GODFREY PHILLIPS
NOVELTY SERIES 1924 C
SET OF 20

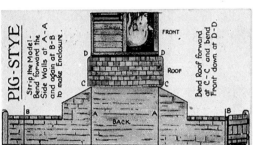

1 DEXTER
  BOROUGH ARMS 1900 B
  SET OF 30

2&3 GODFREY PHILLIPS
  STAMP CARDS 1928 A (each)
  Set length uncertain

4 RECORD CIGARETTE CO
  'TALKIE CARD' 1936 E
  SET OF 25
  (front of card)

5 F & J SMITH
  A TOUR ROUND THE WORLD 1904-5 E
  SET OF 50
  (front of card)

6 WILLS
  SEASIDE RESORTS 1899 E
  SET OF 50

7 PLAYERS
  THE ROYAL FAMILY 1937 A
  Single

8 F & J SMITH
  A TOUR ROUND THE WORLD 1904-5 E
  SET OF 50
  (back of card)

9 CARRERAS
  FILM STARS 1934 B
  SET OF 72

10 WILLS
  CRICKETERS 1896 E
  SET OF 50

11 WILLS
  SHIPS 1895-1902 E
  Sets of 25, 25, and 50

12 MITCHELL
  VILLAGE MODELS 1925 B
  SET OF 25

13,14,15 OGDENS
  CORONATION PROCESS 1937 B
  SET OF 50

These pictures are
CRAYOL
an
KARAM TURK

DRAPKIN'S
CIGARETTES.

DRAPKIN'S
CIGARETTES.

PKIN'S
RETTES.

DRA
CIGAR

DRAPKIN'S
CIGARETTES.

These pictures are only issued with the
CRAYOL VIRGINIA
and
KARAM TURKISH Cigarettes.

DRAPKIN'S
CIGARETTES.

only issued with the
VIRGINIA
nd
KISH Cigarettes.

These pictures are
CRAYOL
a
KARAM TURI

These pictures are only issued with the
CRAYOL VIRGINIA
and
KARAM TURKISH Cigarettes.

DRAPKIN'S
CIGARETTES.

DRAPKIN'S
CIGARETTES.

These pictures are only issued with the
CRAYOL VIRGINIA
and
KARAM TURKISH Cigarettes.

KIN'S
ETTES.

50

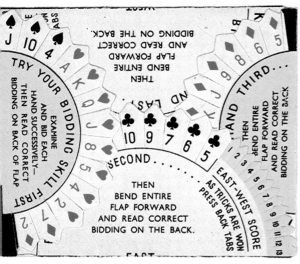

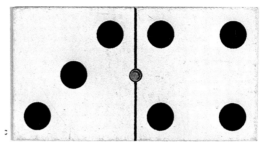

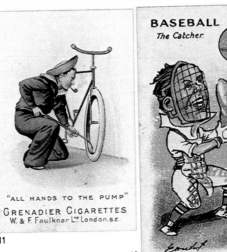

FUN AND GAMES

1&2 COTTON
BRIDGE HANDS 1934 D
SET OF 50

3 COPE & LLOYD (jointly)
GAME OF POKER 1936 A
SET OF 25

4 OGDENS
ABC OF SPORT 1927 B
SET OF 25

5 OGDENS
DOMINOES 1909 B
SET OF 55

6 PLAYERS
EVERYDAY PHRASES 1901 E
SET OF 25

7 CHURCHMAN
HOWLERS 1937 A
SET OF 40

8 WIX
HENRY 1935-7 B
5 SETS OF 50

9 CARRERAS
GREYHOUND RACING GAME 1926 A
SET OF 52

10 SARONY
SARONICKS 1929 A
SET OF 50

11 FAULKNER
NAUTICAL TERMS 1900 D
SET OF 12

12 MAJOR DRAPKIN
THE GAME OF SPORTING SNAP 1928 B
SET OF 40

13 CARRERAS
FORTUNE TELLING 1936 B
SET OF 36

14 WILLS
DOUBLE MEANING 1898 E
SET OF 50

LEAGUE COLOURS

READING

B.D.V. CIGARETTES

DUTCH PRINCESS JULIANA.
BORN 30TH APRIL 1909

Series 30. CITY ARMS B.D.V.
NOTTINGHAM CIGARETTES

S.U. KENTUCKY

ZWITSERLAND
STANDAARD

2 PEACOCK

3RD REGT. VICTORIA RIFLES
MONTREAL.

B.D.V. Cigarettes

38
Henrietta of France Van Dyck

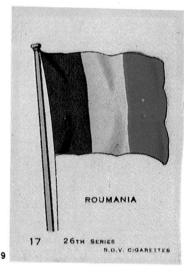

ROUMANIA

17 26TH SERIES
B.D.V. CIGARETTES

ASSORTED SILKS

1 GODFREY PHILLIPS
  FOOTBALL COLOURS 1925 D
  SET OF 90

2 BRITISH AMERICAN TOBACCO
  DUTCH ROYAL FAMILY 1920 B
  SET OF 2

3 GODFREY PHILLIPS
  TOWN & CITY ARMS 1915 C
  SET OF 75

4 AMERICAN TOBACCO
  COLLEGE SEALS 1910 E
  SET OF 143

5 TURMAC (HOLLAND)
  FLAGS & ARMS 1910 E
  SET OF 252

6 GODFREY PHILLIPS
  BRITISH BUTTERFLIES
  & MOTHS 1920 C
  SET OF 50

7 BRITISH AMERICAN TOBACCO
  REGIMENTAL UNIFORMS
  OF CANADA 1920 D
  SET OF 55

8 GODFREY PHILLIPS
  OLD MASTERS 1915 B
  SET OF 60

9 GODFREY PHILLIPS
  FLAGS 1918 B
  SET OF 120

B.D.V.   Cigarettes

34

Portrait of a Child   Rubens

AMARYLLIS
(Beautiful but timid.)

"When Heaven's high vault
condensing clouds
deform
Fair Amaryllis flies the
incumbent storm,
Seeks with unsteady step
the sheltered vale
And turns her blushing
beauty from the gale."
Darwin.

Amaryllis was a beautiful
shepherdess written of by the
Greek and Latin poets
Theocritus and Virgil.
There are several quite
distinct flowers known as
Amaryllis. The true plant is
the Belladonna Lily, so named
because its extract was used to
brighten the eyes and render
the user more beautiful.
Our illustration shows the
Amaryllis of gardens, the St.
Jacob's Lily (Hippeastrum).
This lovely plant was cultivated in England as far back as
1629. The original bulbs came
from South America.

Series 30   TOWN ARMS   B.D.V
ROCHDALE   CIGARETTES

CREDE SIGNO

RED-BACKED SHRIKE
B.D.V. CIGARETTES

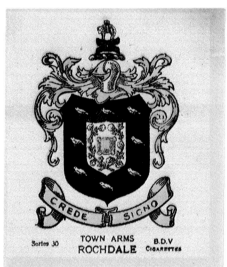

MADAGASCAR

95   15TH SERIES   B.D.V. CIGARETTES

1 GODFREY PHILLIPS
OLD MASTERS 1915 B
SET OF 60

2 ANSTIE
ROYAL STANDARD 1915 A
Single

3 WIX
KENSITAS FLOWERS 1933 B
SET OF 40

4 GODFREY PHILLIPS
TOWN & CITY ARMS 1915 B
SET OF 75

5 ANSTIE
LORD KITCHENER 1915 A
Single

6 HILL
GREAT WAR LEADERS 1915 B
SET OF 23

7 ANSTIE
REGIMENTAL BADGES 1915 D
SET OF 82

8 GODFREY PHILLIPS
BIRDS 1920 E
SET OF 100

9 LEA
REGIMENTAL
CRESTS & BADGES 1920 D
SET OF 100

10 GODFREY PHILLIPS
FLAGS 1915 D
SET OF 75

11 ANONYMOUS (Australia)
1910 A (each)
Set length uncertain

53

METAL FRAMED PHOTOGRAPHS

COHEN WEENEN
CELEBRITIES, GAINSBOROUGH 1901 B (each)
Set length uncertain

CIRCULARS

◁ ROTHMANS
BEAUTIES OF THE CINEMA 1939 A
SET OF 24

ENAMELLED OVAL MINIATURES

WILLS
MINIATURES, OVAL MEDALLIONS 1914 E
SET OF 25

Military

The military theme is perhaps the subject which has appeared most commonly on cards from the earliest issues right through to the present day. Many hundreds of different series have been issued covering medals, ribbons, decorations, regimental colours, badges, banners, orders of chivalry, uniforms, headdress, army corps and divisional signs, arms and armour, weapons, maps, military equipment, air-raid precautions, life in the services, warriors, heroes, military leaders, battle scenes and even regimental pets. There is a very good reason for this. Armed conflict, whether localized or world-wide, has broken out at regular intervals during the last hundred years – the Russo-Japanese War, Boer War, Boxer Rebellion, The Great War and World War II. All have left their mark on cards. And, of course, men, who until recently made up the great majority of smokers, have always been pre-occupied with military matters. The wealth of material to be found on cards is so comprehensive, detailed, and accurate that they are often used for research by military historians.

Among the first cards issued in Britain were a series on Soldiers and Sailors by Wills, and other companies soon discovered the popularity of the theme. The last major war of the 19th Century to involve British troops was the Boer War in South Africa, and this gave special impetus to dozens of firms to produce cards on the subject, in particular on our generals and heroes, because information and pictures of the personalities were readily available from the War Office. One firm, Taddy, even produced a series picturing Boer Leaders. Faulkner also departed from the path trodden by other companies and issued their South African War scenes, as did Goodbody with their With the Flag to Pretoria. Lambert & Butler combined the Boer War and Boxer Rebellion with a series of sketches, and several small firms joined forces to produce a joint series of Boer War Cartoons.

In 1905 Player commemorated the centenary of Trafalgar with Life on Board a Man of War in 1805 and 1905, a beautifully printed comparison of naval life and traditions one hundred years on. But it was the outbreak of the Great War which led to a spate of military issues, and in much greater variety than before. There were the usual straightforward sets of Generals and winners of the Victoria Cross, but also War Pictures, War Maps (Edwards Ringer and Bigg) and Aircraft (used in battle for the first time). Cards were used as an aid in the call to arms, with Wills' set of miniature Recruiting Posters as published by the Parliamentary Recruiting Committee. The mark of censorship was to be found on series, such as Wills Military

Motors bearing the words 'passed by the Censor' with the date.

Politics played a part; Wills prepared a set to commemorate the centenary of Waterloo but it was never issued because of the War alliance with France. The same firm's Musical Celebrities 2nd Series contained eight Germans; these were withdrawn and cards of other nationalities substituted. More subtly, series extolling the beauty of buildings in the front line (Gems of Belgian and Gems of French Architecture by Wills) were produced. The role of Britain's allies was recognized by such series as Wills Allied Army Leaders and Lea's Civilians of Countries Fighting with the Allies. Humour – Martin's 'Arf a 'Mo Kaiser, Hills Fragments From France (by Bruce Bairnsfather) – was used to express the lighter side of life in the trenches, and the cartoonist's brush was enlisted as a propaganda weapon to vilify the enemy, to expose his barbarity and treachery in Wills Punch Cartoons and Carreras Raemaekers War Cartoons.

The war-time shortage of raw materials led to the suspension of cigarette card issues for five years or so. On the resumption in 1922, military issues faded into the background. The 20s was a period when most people wanted to forget the war, and the few issues on this theme tended to be either historical or in the badges and signs category. This trend continued through the early part of the 30s, but as the signs of another major war loomed nearer, tobacco manufacturers became much more prolific in their output of martial material. Apart from the more traditional uniforms and medals, these issues fell into three clearly defined categories: those which emphasized Britain's preparedness for war – Aircraft of the RAF, Modern Naval Craft (both by Players), Britain's Defences (Carreras); those which were designed to give civilians a foretaste of what to expect after mobilization – Life in the Services (Ardath), The Navy at Work, and the RAF at Work (Churchman), Life in the Royal Navy (Wills); and information for civilians – Aircraft (identification) by Godfrey Phillips, Air Raid Precautions (by Wills and other branches of Imperial Tobacco). Whether the Government sought the co-operation of tobacco manufacturers in putting out these series, or the companies merely reflected the nation's mood, is not clear. But these series all served a useful purpose in preparing the population psychologically for war. The last cards to be issued with tobacco (by Ardath in 1941 and 1942) before war shortages again caused a temporary halt, were actually produced by the Ministry of Information and were sloganized cartoons of the 'Careless Words Costs Lives', 'Dig for Victory' style.

"FALL IN"

ANSWER NOW
IN YOUR COUNTRY'S
HOUR OF NEED

REMEMBER BELGIUM

ENLIST TO-DAY

COME ALONG, BOYS!

ENLIST TO-DAY

THE "SCRAP OF PAPER"

ENLIST TO-DAY

THERE IS STILL
A PLACE IN THE LINE
FOR
YOU

THIS SPACE IS RESERVED FOR A FIT MAN

Will you fill it?

RALLY ROUND THE FLAG

"WE MUST HAVE MORE MEN"

Follow me!

YOUR COUNTRY
NEEDS YOU

Another Call

**"MORE
MEN
AND STILL
MORE
UNTIL THE ENEMY
IS CRUSHED"**

LORD KITCHENER.

What in the end will
settle this war?
**TRAINED
MEN**
It is
YOUR DUTY
to become one

LINE UP, BOYS!

ENLIST TO-DAY.

He did his duty.
Will YOU do YOURS?

THINK!

ARE YOU CONTENT FOR
HIM TO FIGHT FOR **YOU**?

WON'T YOU DO YOUR BIT?

WE SHALL WIN
BUT **YOU** MUST HELP

JOIN TO-DAY

WILLS'S CIGARETTES.

GENERAL EVERT.

WILLS'S CIGARETTES.

H.M. KING OF ITALY.

WILLS'S CIGARETTES.

GENERAL SIR L. RUNDLE.

WILLS'S CIGARETTES.

H.I.M. TSAR OF RUSSIA.

WILLS'S CIGARETTES.

LATE F.-M. EARL KITCHENER.

WILLS'S CIGARETTES.

GENERAL AVERESCU.

WILLS'S CIGARETTES.

GENERAL DIMITRIEFF.

WILLS'S CIGARETTES.

GENERAL BRUSILOFF.

WILLS'S CIGARETTES.

GENERAL ZOTTU.

WILLS'S CIGARETTES.

FIELD-MARSHAL SIR D. HAIG.

WILLS'S CIGARETTES.

FIELD-MARSHAL LORD FRENCH.

WILLS'S CIGARETTES.

LT.-GEN. SIR A. J. MURRAY.

WILLS'S CIGARETTES.

GEN. SIR F. R. WINGATE.

WILLS'S CIGARETTES.

H.I.H. GRAND DUKE NICHOLAS.

WILLS'S CIGARETTES.

MARSHAL JOFFRE.

WILLS'S CIGARETTES.

GEN. SIR H. L. SMITH-DORRIEN.

WILLS'S CIGARETTES.

MAHARAJAH SIR PERTAB SINGHJI.

WILLS'S CIGARETTES.

H.M. KING OF MONTENEGRO.

WILLS
ALLIED ARMY LEADERS 1917 C
SET OF 50

WILLS'S CIGARETTES.

H.M. KING OF THE BELGIANS.

WILLS'S CIGARETTES.

GENERAL PÉTAIN.

WILLS'S CIGARETTES.

GENERAL ALEXEIEFF.

WILLS'S CIGARETTES.

GENERAL KOUROPATKIN.

WILLS'S CIGARETTES.

GENERAL RUZSKY.

WILLS'S CIGARETTES.

GENERAL WIELEMANS.

WILLS'S CIGARETTES.

LT.-GEN. SIR P. H. N. LAKE.

WILLS'S CIGARETTES.

LT.-GEN. SIR J. WOLFE MURRAY.

WILLS'S CIGARETTES.

LT.-GEN. SIR W. R. BIRDWOOD.

WILLS'S CIGARETTES.

H.M. KING OF SERBIA.

WILLS'S CIGARETTES.

GENERAL IVANOFF.

WILLS'S CIGARETTES.

H.M. KING OF MONTENEGRO.

WILLS'S CIGARETTES.

GENERAL LECHITSKY.

WILLS'S CIGARETTES.

MAJ.-GEN. SIR C. V. F. TOWNSHEND.

WILLS'S CIGARETTES.

GENERAL SIR C. C. MONRO.

WILLS'S CIGARETTES.

H.R.H. CR. PRINCE OF SERBIA.

WILLS'S CIGARETTES.

FIELD-MARSHAL PUTNIK.

WILLS'S CIGARETTES.

GENERAL SARRAIL.

BRITISH MEDALS & RIBBONS Nº 5.

Waterloo, 1815.

BRITISH MEDALS & RIBBONS Nº 6.

Burmah, 1824-26.

BRITISH MEDALS & RIBBONS Nº 9.

2nd Jellalabad. (Superseding first.)

BRITISH MEDALS & RIBBONS Nº 15.

Gwalior, 1843.

BRITISH MEDALS & RIBBONS Nº 24.

Indian Mutiny, 1857-8.

BRITISH MEDALS & RIBBONS Nº 27.

New Zealand Cross.

BRITISH MEDALS & RIBBONS Nº 30.

South Africa, 1877-79.

BRITISH MEDALS & RIBBONS Nº 31.

Roberts' Star.

BRITISH MEDALS & RIBBONS Nº 32.

Egypt, 1882.

BRITISH MEDALS & RIBBONS Nº 33.

Bronze Star. (Khedive's,) Egypt.

BRITISH MEDALS & RIBBONS Nº 34.

Canada, 1885.

BRITISH MEDALS & RIBBONS Nº 35.

Matabeleland, 1893.

BRITISH MEDALS & RIBBONS Nº 37.

Best Shot. British Army.

BRITISH MEDALS & RIBBONS Nº 38.

Volunteer Officer's Decoration.

BRITISH MEDALS & RIBBONS Nº 40.

Victoria Cross.

BRITISH MEDALS & RIBBONS Nº 41.

Distinguished Service Order.

BRITISH MEDALS & RIBBONS Nº 45.

India Medal, 1895.

BRITISH MEDALS & RIBBONS Nº 46.

Ashanti Star.

V.C. HEROES – BOER WAR.
N.º 42

General Sir Redvers Buller. V.C.
Awarded the Victoria Cross for saving several lives under a terrible fire at Inhlobane Mountain March 28th 1879.

V.C. HEROES – BOER WAR.
N.º 43

Lieu. Gen. Sir George White. V.C.
Awarded the Victoria Cross for conspicuous bravery during the engagement at Charasiah, Afghan War in 1879.

V.C. HEROES – BOER WAR.
N.º 44

The Late Lieut. F. Roberts. V.C.
Awarded the Victoria Cross for his gallant attempt to save the guns at the Battle of Colenso. Dec. 15. 1899.

V.C. HEROES – BOER WAR.
N.º 45

The late Capt. the Hon. R. de Montmorency. V.C.
Awarded the Victoria Cross for bravery in attempting to rescue the body of Lieut. Grenfell who fell in the charge of the 21st Lancer at Omdurman Sep. 2nd 1898.

V.C. HEROES – BOER WAR.
N.º 46.

Lieu. Col. Dick-Cunyngham. V.C.
Awarded the Victoria Cross for valour exhibited during the war in Afghanistan 1879-80.

V.C. HEROES – BOER WAR.
N.º 47

Captain P. A. Kenna. V.C.
Awarded the Victoria Cross for gallantry at the Battle of Khartum 2nd September 1898. He assisted Major Wyndham by taking him on his horse to a place of safety.

V.C. HEROES – BOER WAR.
N.º 48

Captain E. B. Towse. V.C.
Awarded the Victoria Cross for bravery at Magersfontein Dec. 11. 1899, and later at Mount Thaba April 30th 1900.

V.C. HEROES – BOER WAR
N.º 49

Captain Fitzclarence. V.C.
Awarded the Victoria Cross for gallantry at Mafeking on October 14 & 27, executing some wonderful night attacks on the Boer trenches.

V.C. HEROES – BOER WAR
N.º 50

Capt. W. N. Congreve. V.C.
Awarded the Victoria Cross for gallant bravery during the attempt to save the guns at Colenso. 15th Dec. 1899.

V.C. HEROES – BOER WAR.
N.º 51

Capt. H. L. Reed. R. A. V.C.
Awarded the Victoria Cross for gallant bravery during the attempt to save the guns at Colenso, 15. Dec. 1899.

V.C. HEROES – BOER WAR.
N.º 52

Driver H. H. Glassock. V.C.
Awarded the Victoria Cross for bravery exhibited when the Q Battery Royal Horse Artillery saved the guns at Korn Spruit, March 31. 1900.

V.C. HEROES – BOER WAR.
N.º 53

Gunner Isaac Lodge. V.C.
Awarded the Victoria Cross for bravery exhibited when the Q Battery Royal Horse Artillery saved the guns at Korn Spruit, March 31. 1900.

V.C. HEROES – BOER WAR.
N.º 54

Major E. J. Phipps-Hornby. V.C.
Awarded the Victoria Cross for gallantly saving guns at Korn Spruit, March 31. 1900, whilst in command of Q Battery, Royal Horse Artillery.

V.C. HEROES – BOER WAR.
N.º 55

Captain M. F. M. Meiklejohn. V.C.
Awarded the Victoria Cross for gallantly rallying the men of his regiment at Elandslaagte Oct. 21, 1899, whilst badly wounded.

V.C. HEROES – BOER WAR.
N.º 56

Capt. Sir J. P. Milbanke. V.C.
Awarded the Victoria Cross for gallantry near Colesberg. January 5th 1900. Under a galling fire he rescued a trooper left on battlefield.

V.C. HEROES – BOER WAR.
N.º 57

Lieutenant Robertson. V.C.
Awarded the Victoria Cross for gallantry displayed at Elandslaagte October 21st 1900 whilst dangerously wounded.

V.C. HEROES – BOER WAR.
N.º 58

Capt. N. M. Smyth. V.C.
Awarded the Victoria Cross for bravery at the Battle of Khartum. Sep. 2nd 1898. He intercepted the charge of an Arab who had got amongst our camp followers, killing the Arab himself being wounded in the arm.

V.C. HEROES – BOER WAR.
N.º 59

Major W. Babtie. V.C.
Of the Royal Army Medical Corps was awarded the Victoria Cross for gallantry at Battle of Colenso. Under heavy fire he attended to many wounded soldiers.

TADDY
VC HEROES 1902 D
SET OF 20
Between 1901 and 1904 Taddy issued 6 sets
of VC Heroes making 125 cards in all.

SEARCHLIGHT SECTION.

CYCLIST SCOUT SECTION.

LANCE V. SWORD.

FIRING FROM GUN PIT.

FILTERING WATER.

MAP READING CLASS.

STARTING THE ENGINE.

UNPACKING WAGGON.

LAYING A FIELD TELEGRAPH LINE.

WAR KITE DRILL.

LAMP SIGNALLING.

BRINGING IN WOUNDED MAN.

BALLOON DRILL.

FLAG SIGNALLING.

JUMPING WITH LED HORSE.

PICKING UP WOUNDED.

BAYONET FIGHTING.

MECHANICAL TRANSPORT SECTION.

PLAYERS
ARMY LIFE 1910 B
SET OF 25

WILLS ▷
MILITARY MOTORS 1916 B
SET OF 50
Two sets were issued in the same year.
One with the words 'Passed by Censor'
to indicate that classified information was not being passed
to the enemy.

WILL'S CIGARETTES.
MOTOR MITRAILLEUSE.

WILL'S CIGARETTES.
MOTOR RAFT.

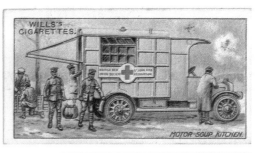

WILL'S CIGARETTES.
MOTOR SOUP KITCHEN.

WILL'S CIGARETTES.
MOTOR SEARCHLIGHT.

WILL'S CIGARETTES.
MOTOR CYCLE MAXIM.

WILL'S CIGARETTES.
MOTOR BUS.

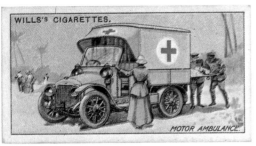

WILL'S CIGARETTES.
MOTOR AMBULANCE.

WILL'S CIGARETTES.
MOTOR SEARCHLIGHT.

WILL'S CIGARETTES.
MOTOR LORRY.

WILL'S CIGARETTES.
ARMOURED CAR.

WILL'S CIGARETTES.
OFFICER'S SIDE CAR.

WILL'S CIGARETTES.
ARMOURED CARS.

WILL'S CIGARETTES.
MOTOR WIRE CUTTER.

WILL'S CIGARETTES.
ARMOURED CARS.

WILL'S CIGARETTES.
KING VICTOR'S CAR.

WILL'S CIGARETTES.
ARMOURED TRICYCLE.

WILL'S CIGARETTES.
MOTOR BUSES.

WILL'S CIGARETTES.
FLYING CORPS MOTOR.

WILL'S CIGARETTES.
MOTOR AUTO-GUN.

WILL'S CIGARETTES.
MOTOR PIGEON-COTE.

WILL'S CIGARETTES.
MOTOR KITCHEN.

PLAYER'S CIGARETTES.

21st FUSILIERS REGT. OF FOOT;
Officer's full dress shako, 1844.

PLAYER'S CIGARETTES.

7TH
(QUEEN'S OWN)
HUSSARS;
Officer's full dress shako, 1807.

PLAYER'S CIGARETTES.

50TH RIFLES.
(THE KING'S ROYAL RIFLE CORPS);
Officer's full dress busby, 1873-78.

PLAYER'S CIGARETTES.

7TH (QUEEN'S OWN) HUSSARS;
Officer's full dress busby, 1815.

PLAYER'S CIGARETTES.

91ST REGIMENT OF FOOT;
Officer's full dress shako, 1816.

PLAYER'S CIGARETTES.

37TH REGIMENT OF FOOT;
Major's full dress shako, 1861-69.

PLAYER'S CIGARETTES.

25TH REGIMENT OF FOOT;
Officer's full dress shako, 1869-78.

PLAYER'S CIGARETTES.

4TH REGIMENT OF FOOT;
Officer's forage cap, 1852-1881.

PLAYER'S CIGARETTES.

INFANTRY PRIVATE'S SHAKO,
1800-1806.

PLAYER'S CIGARETTES.

INFANTRY OFFICER'S SHAKO;
1811-16.

PLAYER'S CIGARETTES.

17TH REGIMENT OF FOOT;
Officer's full dress helmet, 1879-81.

PLAYER'S CIGARETTES.

THE RIFLE BRIGADE;
Officer's full dress shako, 1829-44.

PLAYER'S CIGARETTES.

15TH THE KING'S HUSSARS;
Officer's full dress busby, 1881.

PLAYER'S CIGARETTES.

43RD REGIMENT OF FOOT;
Private's forage cap, 1852.

PLAYER'S CIGARETTES.

9TH (QUEEN'S ROYAL) LANCERS;
Officer's full dress cap, 1830-40.

PLAYER'S CIGARETTES.

93RD REGIMENT OF FOOT;
Bandsman's forage cap, 1849.

PLAYER'S CIGARETTES.

19TH LANCERS;
Officer's full dress cap, 1820.

PLAYER'S CIGARETTES.

15TH THE KING'S HUSSARS;
Officer's full dress shako, 1834.

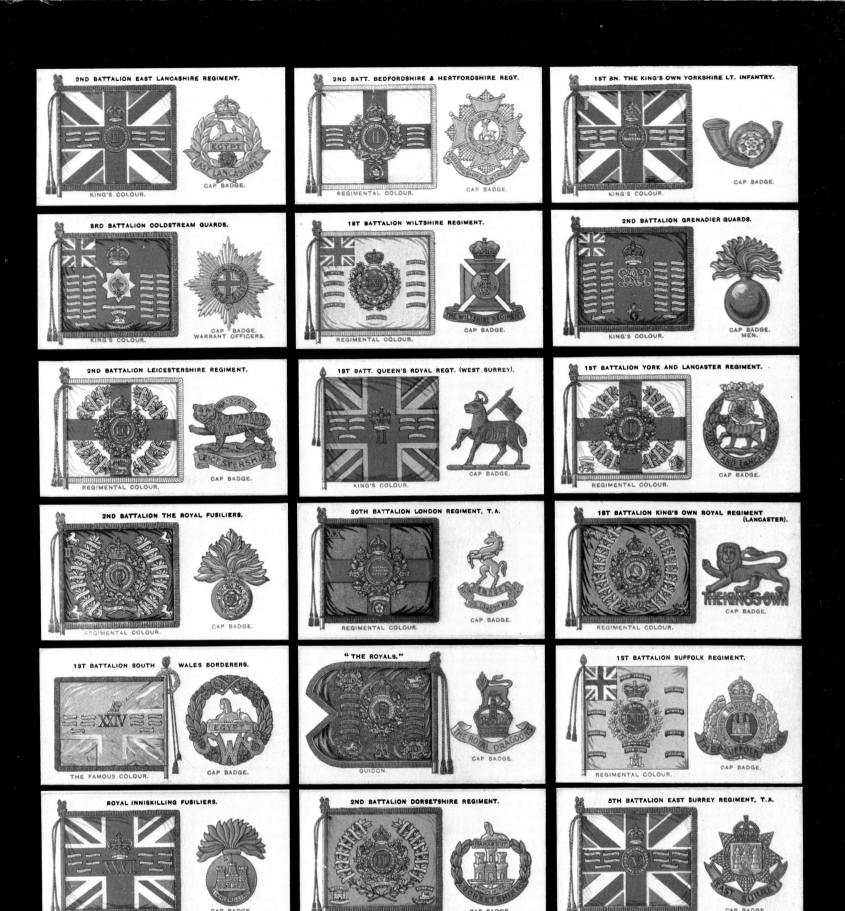

WILL'S CIGARETTES.

ADMIRAL.

WILL'S CIGARETTES.

CAPTAIN.

WILL'S CIGARETTES.

FLEET-SURGEON.

WILL'S CIGARETTES.

COMMANDER.

WILL'S CIGARETTES.

CHIEF GUNNER.

WILL'S CIGARETTES.

CHIEF ARTIFICER ENGINEER.

WILL'S CIGARETTES.

LIEUTENANT, R.N.V.R.

WILL'S CIGARETTES.

2ND CLASS COMMODORE.

WILL'S CIGARETTES.

TORPEDO COXSWAIN.

WILL'S CIGARETTES.

STOKER.

WILL'S CIGARETTES.

STAFF-PAYMASTER.

WILL'S CIGARETTES.

GUNLAYER, 3RD CLASS.

WILL'S CIGARETTES.

ADMIRAL OF THE FLEET.

WILL'S CIGARETTES.

ROYAL MARINE ARTILLERY.

WILL'S CIGARETTES.

LIEUTENANT, R.N.R.

WILL'S CIGARETTES.

SIGNALMAN.

WILL'S CIGARETTES.

LIEUTENANT, OVER 8 YEARS.

WILL'S CIGARETTES.

PETTY OFFICER.

WILLS
NAVAL DRESS & BADGES 1909 C
SET OF 50

FLIGHT MECHANICS REFUELLING AEROPLANE IN DESERT

FLIGHT RIGGERS RECEIVING INSTRUCTION ON SKELETON AIRFRAME

SHORT "SUNDERLAND" FLYING-BOAT

LOWERING FLOAT-PLANE ON TO SEA

FITTERS AND RIGGERS INSPECTING FAIREY "BATTLE"

FLIGHT RIGGERS "TOPPING-UP" OLEO-LEG

FLIGHT RIGGERS UNDER INSTRUCTION AT HENLOW

FITTERS (TORPEDO) WHEELING TORPEDO INTO POSITION

AIRMAN SWINGING THE AIRSCREW

MAINTENANCE OF ENGINE AND TESTING WIRELESS SET

ARMY CO-OPERATION AEROPLANE PICKING UP MESSAGE

FITTERS INSPECTING VICKERS "WELLESLEY" BOMBER

FABRIC WORKERS COVERING WING

FLIGHT MECHANICS INSTALLING ENGINE INTO AIRFRAME

OVERSEAS MOTOR TRANSPORT FITTERS REPAIRING R.A.F. CAR

WILLS'S CIGARETTES

EQUIPPING YOUR REFUGE ROOM—A

WILLS'S CIGARETTES

EQUIPPING YOUR REFUGE ROOM—B

WILLS'S CIGARETTES

A GARDEN DUG-OUT

WILLS'S CIGARETTES

THE CIVILIAN DUTY RESPIRATOR

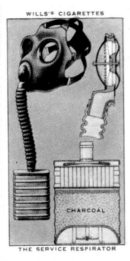
WILLS'S CIGARETTES

THE SERVICE RESPIRATOR

WILLS'S CIGARETTES

AIR RAID PRECAUTIONS BADGE

WILLS'S CIGARETTES

A HEAVY ANTI-GAS SUIT

WILLS'S CIGARETTES

THE CIVILIAN RESPIRATOR—HOW TO REMOVE IT

WILLS'S CIGARETTES

PROTECTING YOUR WINDOWS—A SANDBAG DEFENCE

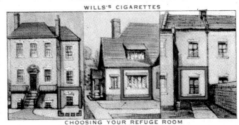
WILLS'S CIGARETTES

CHOOSING YOUR REFUGE ROOM

WILLS'S CIGARETTES

RENDERING YOUR REFUGE ROOM GAS-PROOF

WILLS'S CIGARETTES

WINDOW PROTECTION AGAINST BLAST

WILLS'S CIGARETTES

MAKING A DOOR GAS-PROOF

WILLS'S CIGARETTES

A VENTILATED GAS-PROOF SHELTER

WILLS'S CIGARETTES

WINDOW PROTECTION

WILLS'S CIGARETTES

INCENDIARY BOMB AND ITS EFFECT

WILLS'S CIGARETTES

MEDIUM TRAILER FIRE-PUMP

WILLS'S CIGARETTES

HOSE-LAYING LORRY

WILLS'S CIGARETTES

AIR RAID WARDENS AND CIVILIAN VOLUNTEER DESPATCH-RIDER

◁ CHURCHMAN
RAF AT WORK 1938 B
SET OF 48

WILLS (& OTHERS)
AIR RAID PRECAUTIONS 1938 A
SET OF 40

Sports & Pastimes

Interest in sport is always topical and so was ideally suited to representation on cards. Pictures and information were readily available too as clubs and individuals were glad to get the publicity. The ever changing scene lent itself to the brief production runs that typify card issues, and the way was paved for later updated series. Add to this the fact that the majority of the male population is fanatically interested in one sport or another and it is small wonder this subject has a very prominent place in card issues throughout their history.

Among the earliest sports issues was Wills Cricketers (1896), and their Sports of All Nations (1900). The latter is particularly interesting because it shows contemporary sports dress and equipment; freedom of movement was sacrificed in the interests of decorum, particularly evident in the lawn tennis picture where men and women players are heavily encumbered by several layers of clothing. This series includes many sports which would not appear today – coaching, kangaroo driving and lion hunting. It is worth noting the sports appearing most commonly on cards at the turn of the century, because this probably gives a fairly reliable indication of their popularity at that time. Cricket, football (both association and rugby), cycling, boxing, horse-racing and golf are well to the fore. Series covering sport in general tended to have a high proportion of huntin', shootin' and fishin' – wild fowling, salmon fishing, pheasant shooting, pig-sticking, coursing and otter-hunting. Topics which had almost disappeared from cards after the First World War.

Sporting themes were prominent, too, in card issues from Australia. The major British firms exported their most popular series but, in addition, there were favourite local issues from firms like Snider and Abrahams. Their cards covered series like the 'Australian Cricket Team 1905', 'Australian Football Incidents in Play' and 'Australian Jockeys'. Cricket series, in particular, were prominent contributing to the fact that there are over eleven thousand cards which can be collected on this sport. The British American Tobacco Company issued many sporting series before the Great War. Through its international trading activities the company was responsible for many indigenous sets; from Canada came the national game of lacrosse, baseball from the States, even European footballers found their way into the cards issued. Any historian tracing the international development of sport would find the cards and novelties a mine of fascinating information.

In the inter-war years, sport was a major source of inspiration for card issuers. Soccer and cricket dominated the scene. Rugby, boxing, horse-racing and golf were still popular, but cycling had faded into the background. The range of sports having entire series of cards devoted to them had widened considerably. Most remarkable was the number of issues on tennis due in no small measure to the tremendous influence that Wimbledon had on the public's imagination in the 1930s. 'New' sports were attracting the crowds, and greyhound racing, speedway, motor racing or motor cycling all found a place in card issues, as did swimming, billiards, pigeon racing, hurling and yachting.

Godfrey Phillips marked the 1928 Olympics in Amsterdam with a special series. But football was the subject most depicted. Ardath issued hundreds of team photographs during the six months from August 1936; even obscure amateur clubs were included. Other firms did series on football players, captains, records, club nicknames, F.A. cup winners, and hints on the game; there were head and shoulder portraits, full-length pictures, action shots, drawings and caricatures. There were sets depicting sporting personalities, events, and trophies. Ogdens issued a humorous ABC of Sport. Royalty were shown taking part in various sports, and in attendance as spectators or presenting cups. Live outside broadcasts from sporting events are illustrated, and there is mention even of television coverage of Wimbledon (Churchman Modern Wonders 1938). Famous cartoonists were commissioned to produce caricatures of the great players, artists and photographers were employed to capture the excitement of sportsmen in action, galleries were approached for permission to reproduce paintings of historic events and bygone winners, famous sportsmen were engaged to demonstrate their strokes, skills and techniques, all to be portrayed on cards.

Since the war, among trade issues, the number of sporting series has intensified. Football still retains its prime position. Some firms, such as A.& B.C. and Topps, have made it their task to issue large series of 300 or more pictures of footballers annually; others have concentrated on particular aspects such as clubs and badges, coaching or the World Cup. Cricket has also been well to the fore and Top Trumps are now issuing two series, British and International, each year. Other sports to have been featured include athletics, water sports, motor cycling, motor racing, the Olympics, rugby and tennis, and there have been numerous general series on sports, sportsmen, and sporting trophies.

OGDEN'S CIGARETTES.

CENTURIONS.

OGDEN'S CIGARETTES.

Ladies.

Gentlemen.

BROOKLANDS AUTOMOBILE
RACING CLUB.

OGDEN'S CIGARETTES.

BRITISH SEA ANGLERS' SOCIETY.

OGDEN'S CIGARETTES.

AMATEUR SWIMMING CLUB.

OGDEN'S CIGARETTES.

NEWPORT ATHLETIC CLUB.

OGDEN'S CIGARETTES.

CITY AND SUBURBAN HARRIERS.

OGDEN'S CIGARETTES.

AMATEUR DIVING ASSOCIATION.

OGDEN'S CIGARETTES.

CORNWALL COUNTY HOCKEY
ASSOCIATION.

OGDEN'S CIGARETTES.

HALLAMSHIRE HARRIERS.

OGDEN'S CIGARETTES.

HERTS. COUNTY AUTOMOBILE
AND AERO CLUB.

OGDEN'S CIGARETTES.

IRISH AMATEUR ATHLETIC
ASSOCIATION.

OGDEN'S CIGARETTES.

LEICESTER BICYCLE CLUB (REG)

OGDEN'S CIGARETTES.

LONDON ATHLETIC CLUB.

OGDEN'S CIGARETTES.

ROYAL CINQUE PORTS YACHT
CLUB.

OGDEN'S CIGARETTES.

AMATEUR CAMPING CLUB.

OGDEN'S CIGARETTES.

MANX AUTOMOBILE CLUB.

OGDEN'S CIGARETTES.

ULSTERVILLE HARRIER CLUB.

OGDEN'S CIGARETTES.

THAMES HARE AND HOUNDS.

WILLS'S CIGARETTES.
WILLS'S CIGARETTES.
WILLS'S CIGARETTES.
WILLS'S CIGARETTES.
WILLS'S CIGARETTES.
WILLS'S CIGARETTES.

A. FIELDER (KENT).

G. J. THOMPSON (NORTHAMPTON.).

MR. A. C. MACLAREN (LANCS.).

J. HARDSTAFF (NOTTS.).

W. EAST (NORTHAMPTONSHIRE).

J. H. BOARD (GLOUCESTERSHIRE).

WILLS'S CIGARETTES.
WILLS'S CIGARETTES.
WILLS'S CIGARETTES.
WILLS'S CIGARETTES.
WILLS'S CIGARETTES.
WILLS'S CIGARETTES.

A. R. WARREN (DERBYSHIRE).

MR. C. B. FRY (SUSSEX).

E. G. HAYES (SURREY)

T. HAYWARD (SURREY).

JOHN GUNN (NOTTS.).

MR. C. J. B. WOOD (LEICESTER).

WILLS'S CIGARETTES.
WILLS'S CIGARETTES.
WILLS'S CIGARETTES.
WILLS'S CIGARETTES.
WILLS'S CIGARETTES.
WILLS'S CIGARETTES.

MR. G. N. FOSTER (WORCESTER.).

A. STONE (HAMPSHIRE).

G. COX (SUSSEX).

J. SHARP (LANCASHIRE).

MR. PERCY A. PERRIN (ESSEX).

C. BLYTHE (KENT).

WILLS
CRICKETERS 1908 D
SET OF 50

S. F. BARNES (STAFFORDSHIRE).

ALBERT W. HALLAM (NOTTS.).

MR. C. H. B. MARSHAM (KENT).

MR. H. K. FOSTER (WORCESTER).

MR. E. M. SPROT (HAMPSHIRE).

L. C. BRAUND (SOMERSET).

MR. C. P. McGAHEY (ESSEX).

MR. P. F. WARNER (MIDDLESEX).

G. GUNN (NOTTINGHAMSHIRE).

MR. G. L. JESSOP (GLO'STER.).

MR. K. L. HUTCHINGS (KENT).

A. A. LILLEY (WARWICKSHIRE).

J. HUMPHRIES (DERBYSHIRE).

A. E. RELF (SUSSEX).

MR. A. O. JONES (NOTTS.).

LORD HAWKE (YORKSHIRE).

J. B. HOBBS (SURREY).

A. E. LEWIS (SOMERSET.).

CHURCHMAN'S CIGARETTES	CHURCHMAN'S CIGARETTES	CHURCHMAN'S CIGARETTES	CHURCHMAN'S CIGARETTES	CHURCHMAN'S CIGARETTES	CHURCHMAN'S CIGARETTES
T. BROLLY (MILLWALL)	G. W. HALL (TOTTENHAM HOTSPUR)	P. GROSVENOR (LEICESTER CITY)	T. JOHNSON (SHEFFIELD UNITED)	V. WOODLEY (CHELSEA)	J. PAYNE (CHELSEA)

CHURCHMAN'S CIGARETTES	CHURCHMAN'S CIGARETTES	CHURCHMAN'S CIGARETTES	CHURCHMAN'S CIGARETTES	CHURCHMAN'S CIGARETTES	CHURCHMAN'S CIGARETTES
J. R. MARTIN (ASTON VILLA)	R. TOMLINSON (SOUTHAMPTON)	A. E. STEVENSON (EVERTON)	J. JAMES (BRENTFORD)	G. TADMAN (CHARLTON ATHLETIC)	F. C. STEELE (STOKE CITY)

CHURCHMAN'S CIGARETTES	CHURCHMAN'S CIGARETTES	CHURCHMAN'S CIGARETTES	CHURCHMAN'S CIGARETTES	CHURCHMAN'S CIGARETTES	CHURCHMAN'S CIGARETTES
W. FAGAN (LIVERPOOL)	S. MATTHEWS (STOKE CITY)	L. GOLDBERG (LEEDS UNITED)	W. MORRIS (WOLVERHAMPTON WANDERERS)	W. SHANKLY (PRESTON NORTH END)	H. CLIFTON (NEWCASTLE UNITED)

CHURCHMAN'S CIGARETTES	CHURCHMAN'S CIGARETTES	CHURCHMAN'S CIGARETTES	CHURCHMAN'S CIGARETTES	CHURCHMAN'S CIGARETTES	CHURCHMAN'S CIGARETTES
R. DAVIDSON (COVENTRY CITY)	S. BARTRAM (CHARLTON ATHLETIC)	J. HODGSON (GRIMSBY TOWN)	I. M. HOPKINS (BRENTFORD)	J. BROWN (BIRMINGHAM)	W. E. HAYES (HUDDERSFIELD TOWN)

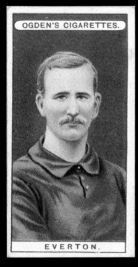

EVERTON.

GLOUCESTER.

SWANSEA.

RICHMOND.

BRISTOL.

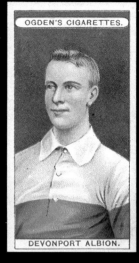

DEVONPORT ALBION.

BLACKHEATH.

ASTON VILLA.

W'HAMPTON WANDERERS.

NOTTS. FOREST.

NEWCASTLE UNITED.

WATFORD.

BLACKBURN ROVERS.

NORTHAMPTON.

MIDDLESBROUGH.

TOTTENHAM HOTSPUR.

SHEFFIELD UNITED.

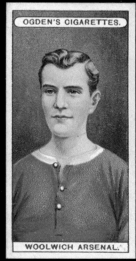

WOOLWICH ARSENAL.

◁ CHURCHMAN
ASSOCIATION FOOTBALLERS 2ND SERIES 1939 A
SET OF 50

OGDENS
FOOTBALL CLUB COLOURS 1906 C
SET OF 51

EPSOM LAD.

GALOPIN.

PERDITA II.

MELTON.

ISINGLASS.

MANIFESTO.

SPEARMINT.

SLIEVE GALLION.

IMARI.

SCEPTRE.

ASCETIC'S SILVER.

MOIFAA.

SANTOI.

LA FLÉCHE.

GORGOS.

CHERRY LASS.

KIRKLAND.

VOLODYOVSKI.

OGDENS
RACEHORSES 1907 C
SET OF 50

OGDEN'S CIGARETTES

H. JELLIS — MR. LEONARD BRASSEY
WM. GRIGGS — SIR R. B. JARDINE
F. RICKABY — LORD WOLVERTON

H. JELLIS — COL. E. W. BAIRD
E. PIPER — CAPT. FRANK FORESTER
S. DONOGHUE — CAPT. D. McCALMONT

H. JELLIS — LD. HOWARD DE WALDEN
WAL GRIGGS — MAJOR E. LODER
F. TEMPLEMAN — LORD VILLIERS

S. DONOGHUE — LORD CARNARVON
W. SAXBY — MR. W. RAPHAEL
D. MAHER — MR. FAIRIE

W. HIGGS — MR. S. B. JOEL
D. MAHER — MR. ERNEST TANNER
J. CLARK — EARL OF DURHAM

J. H. MARTIN — SIR WM. COOKE
C. FOY — MR. E. DRESDEN
M. JONES — H.M. THE KING

FRANKLYN'S CIGARETTES.

Position.

FRANKLYN'S CIGARETTES.

Inside guard with left.

FRANKLYN'S CIGARETTES.

Avoiding a right lead and cross-countering with right upper cut.

FRANKLYN'S CIGARETTES.

Guarding right lead at head from outside and countering with right at body.

FRANKLYN'S CIGARETTES.

Stepping inside a left lead and countering with right at body.

FRANKLYN'S CIGARETTES.

Outside guard with left.

FRANKLYN'S CIGARETTES.

Guarding right lead at head with the left and being ready to counter at head or body with right.

FRANKLYN'S CIGARETTES.

Side stepping a left lead and countering with left at the body.

FRANKLYN'S CIGARETTES.

Guarding a left lead and countering with left at body.

FRANKLYN'S CIGARETTES.

Improper left hand lead at the body and stop for same.

FRANKLYN'S CIGARETTES.

Stopping left hand body lead and being ready to counter with left at head or body.

FRANKLYN'S CIGARETTES.

The cross-parry.

FRANKLYN'S CIGARETTES.

Ducking a right lead at head and countering with right at body.

FRANKLYN'S CIGARETTES.

Left hand lead at head.

FRANKLYN'S CIGARETTES.

Avoiding a left lead at head and cross-countering with right upper-cut.

FRANKLYN'S CIGARETTES.

Stopping a left lead from outside and standing ready to cross-counter with the left at the body.

FRANKLYN'S CIGARETTES.

Ducking a left lead and countering with the right at body.

FRANKLYN'S CIGARETTES.

Stopping right lead at body and countering with right at jaw.

78

FRANKLYN DAVEY (& OTHERS)
BOXING 1924 A
SET OF 25

PLAYERS ▷
CYCLING 1939 A
SET OF 50

LADY'S PEDESTRIAN HOBBY-HORSE

PEDESTRIAN HOBBY-HORSE

POST OFFICE CENTRE-CYCLES

"SALVO" TRICYCLE

COMPANION SAFETY BICYCLE

"INVINCIBLE" BICYCLE

"INVINCIBLE" TANDEM TRICYCLE

BICYCLE OF THE LATE '90s

SIMPSON LEVER CHAIN

A NOTABLE TRICYCLIST—
F. T. BIDLAKE

SOCIABLE TRICYCLE

OLYMPIA TANDEM TRICYCLE

ITALIAN VELOCINO BICYCLE

TANDEM OF THE '90s

LADY CYCLIST WEARING
DIVIDED SKIRT

MASSED-START RACING POSITION

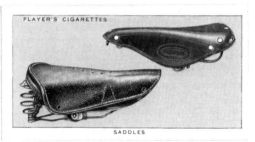
SADDLES

PACING TRIPLET

TRACK TANDEM POSITION

HORIZONTAL BICYCLE

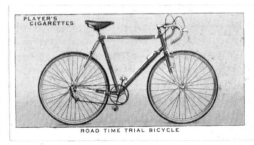
ROAD TIME TRIAL BICYCLE

ABE MITCHELL

T. H. COTTON

DIANA FISHWICK

JOYCE WETHERED

CHARLES WHITCOMBE

PERCY ALLISS

JEAN BOROTRA

HELEN WILLS-MOODY

HELEN JACOBS

PEGGY SCRIVEN

W. T. TILDEN

HENRI COCHET

HAROLD LARWOOD

J. B. HOBBS

FRANK WOOLLEY

J. C. WHITE

WALTER HAMMOND

D. R. JARDINE

ARDATH
CRICKET TENNIS & GOLF CELEBRITIES 1935 A
SET OF 50

WILLS ▷
PHYSICAL CULTURE 1914 B
SET OF 50

81

Stage, Screen and Radio

Cigarette cards faithfully reflect the changes that have occurred during the past hundred years, and the field of entertainment is no exception. At the beginning, the stage, particularly the music hall, was the medium for mass-entertainment, and the stars featured prominently on cards. But towards the end of the nineteenth century, the invention of the Kinetoscope paved the way for the first motion picture theatres. At first the actors and actresses were anonymous; most had defected from the stage and felt that appearing in films was something of a comedown. The only means audiences had of identifying their favourite performers was by association with the various film companies, of which Vitagraph, Biograph and Essanay were the leaders.

1911 saw the forerunner of the true full-length feature films with a three-reel version of A Tale of Two Cities co-starring 'Vitagraph Girl' Florence Turner and the screen's first matinee idol, Maurice Costello. In the previous year, 'Biograph Girl' Florence Lawrence's move to the Independent Motion Picture Co. was turned into a publicity stunt which led to her being mobbed wherever she went. Other companies promptly released the names of their players and the star system was born.

Miss Lawrence's successor as 'Biograph Girl' was an unknown seventeen-year-old actress, Mary Pickford, destined to rocket to stardom and to be immortalised as the World's Sweetheart. In 1919 she became the most powerful woman in the film industry by founding the United Artists film company together with Chaplin, D.W. Griffith, and her future husband Douglas Fairbanks Snr. Most of the great names from the formative days are included in one of the earliest series devoted entirely to film stars, Drapkin's set of 96 Cinematograph Actors (and actresses) issued in 1913.

After the First World War, the cinema continued to gain in popularity, gradually banishing the stage to second place on the card issues of the day. Among the last to feature stars of the silent screen were two series each of 25 cards put out by Wills in 1928. Because the most revolutionary development since Edison invented the Kinetoscope had at last been perfected, the talking picture. As far back as the 1890s attempts had been made to harness another of Edison's brain-children, the phonograph, to give voices to the characters flickering across the screen, but it was not until 1927 that the first successful sound film, The Jazz Singer starring Al Jolson, made the talkies a reality. Almost overnight, the careers of many of the most popular movie stars were in ruins. They could not make the change because of heavy foreign accents or unsuitable speaking voices. And so when Wills issued their third series of Cinema Stars in 1931, most of the old names had vanished to be replaced by newcomers such as Laurel and Hardy, Will Rogers, Joel McCrea, Jeanette Macdonald and Robert Montgomery.

In the early days of sound, film-makers were hampered by the need to enclose the camera in a sound-proof booth, with the result that the first talkies often had the appearance of filmed stage productions. By 1934, when Players issued their first series of Film Stars, technical advances gave directors the freedom to create the fluid and stylish films for which the 30s has become famous in cinema history. And a new generation of superstars – Garbo, Dietrich, Harlow, Hepburn, Cooper, Crawford, Davis, Gable – was being idolized by the millions who flocked each week to queue outside the new cathedrals of entertainment that mushroomed in towns and cities all over the world.

Hundreds of different series of cards featuring film stars were issued in Britain during the 1930s. Photographs, paintings and caricatures by the ton flooded from the presses and into pockets every week. The demand was insatiable. There remained just one major refinement before films were to become as we know them today: colour photography; and that process was perfected in 1938.

Already during the 30s, the cinema's pre-eminence as the king of entertainment was being foreshadowed by the growth of broadcasting. The wireless rapidly found a place in virtually every home in the land, and radio stars began to feature on cards. As early as 1934, some firms, such as Wills, produced whole series devoted to radio celebrities, whilst others, amongst them Ardath, preferred a wider field and issued composite series of Film, Stage and Radio Stars. The real threat to the cinema, though, was still some way off. Television was then in its infancy but its potential was recognized, at least in some quarters. Stephen Mitchell in their series of cards, The World of Tomorrow, issued in 1936, were prophetic about the role television was to play in the future: *'Already television is in use very successfully on a small scale, and it may develop still further. Images of people or events would then be transmitted far and wide to be reproduced in life-like colours. They might be received on a screen at the front of the ordinary wireless receiving set, or on a smaller dial, like that of a watch, carried in the pocket or on the wrist. In public places they might even be projected to appear in more than life-size, high above the heads of the crowd. The images would appear free from haziness or flicker, and the broadcast voices would be free from distortion.'*

MARLENE DIETRICH

NOEL COWARD

NORMA SHEARER

MYRNA LOY

HENRY HALL

CLAUDETTE COLBERT

ANONA WINN

GINGER ROGERS

STANLEY HOLLOWAY

84

CHARLES LAUGHTON

KATHARINE HEPBURN

CLARK GABLE

GEORGE ARLISS

GRACIE FIELDS

KAY FRANCIS

GRETA GARBO

SIR CEDRIC HARDWICKE

ARDATH
FILM, STAGE & RADIO STARS 1935 A
SET OF 25

85

Marika Rökk

Gustav Fröhlich

Lilian Harvey

Monette Dinay

Annabella

Pat Paterson

Jean Harlow

Marlene Dietrich

Joan Crawford

Hilde Hildebrand

Rotraut Richter

Brigitte Helm

Käthe von Nagy

Gustav Fröhlich

Grett Theimer

Marlene Dietrich

WHOSE PIERCING EYES ARE THESE?

THOSE EYES—SURELY YOU KNOW THEM?

SUCH CLASSIC BEAUTY—WHO IS SHE?

PROVOCATIVE AND TANTALISING—WHO?

YOU KNOW THIS ADORABLE FACE?

DETERMINED LIPS—RESOLUTE EYES—WHOSE ARE THEY?

SINCERITY IS IN HER SMILE—WHO IS SHE?

WHOSE SOULFUL EYES AND WISTFUL SMILE?

FIRM LIPS, HUMOROUS EYES—WHOSE?

WISTFUL APPEALING BEAUTY—WHO IS SHE?

EVERYBODY'S FAVOURITE—NAME PLEASE?

PERFECT BUTLER, PERFECT "KING"—WHO IS HE?

WHO IS THE WORLD'S SWEETHEART?

GLORIOUS VOICE—INFECTIOUS SMILE—WHOSE?

WHO IS THIS FAMOUS SCREEN STAR?

YOU RECOGNISE THIS BEWITCHING SMILE?

STRONG COMPELLING FEATURES—WHOSE?

BEAUTY COMBINED WITH TALENT—WHO IS IT?

◁ GARBATY
MODERN BEAUTY GALLERY 1930 A
SET OF 300
A colourful set of hand-coloured photographs
issued in Kurmark cigarettes before the War.

ARDATH
WHO IS THIS? 1936 A
SET OF 50

Norma Shearer

Maureen O'Sullivan

Ronald Colman

Myrna Loy

Gene Reynolds

Tyrone Power

James Stewart

Ida Lupino

Una Merkel

Claudette Colbert

Frances Dee

Gail Patrick

Fredric March

Leslie Howard

Cecilia Parker

Rosalind Russell

Jeanette MacDonald

George Raft

Mickey Rooney

Joan Crawford

Robert Donat

Ray Milland

Robert Montgomery

Herbert Marshall

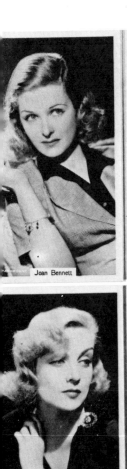

Joan Bennett

Basil Rathbone

Fred MacMurray

Bing Crosby

William Powell

Mary Carlisle

Carole Lombard

Marlene Dietrich

Lloyd Nolan

Luise Rainer

Spencer Tracy

Clark Gable

Charles Boyer

Mary Ellis

Madge Evans

Dorothy Lamour

Eleanor Powell

Gary Cooper

Olympe Bradna

Janet Gaynor

Eileen Drew

Randolph Scott

Nelson Eddy

R J LEA
FAMOUS FILM STARS 1939 A
SET OF 54

CHARLES RAY.

RAMON NOVARRO.

LILLIAN GISH.

CLIVE BROOK.

IVOR NOVELLO.

BEBE DANIELS.

CONSTANCE TALMADGE.

WILLIAM BOYD.

DOLORES COSTELLO.

MARGUERITE DE LA MOTTE.

HAROLD LLOYD.

RICHARD DIX.

RICARDO CORTEZ.

MARION DAVIES.

LEW CODY.

JOHN GILBERT.

SYD CHAPLIN.

TOM MIX.

WILLS
CINEMA STARS 1ST SERIES 1928 A
SET OF 25

LAMBERT & BUTLER ▷
DANCE BAND LEADERS 1936 A
SET OF 25

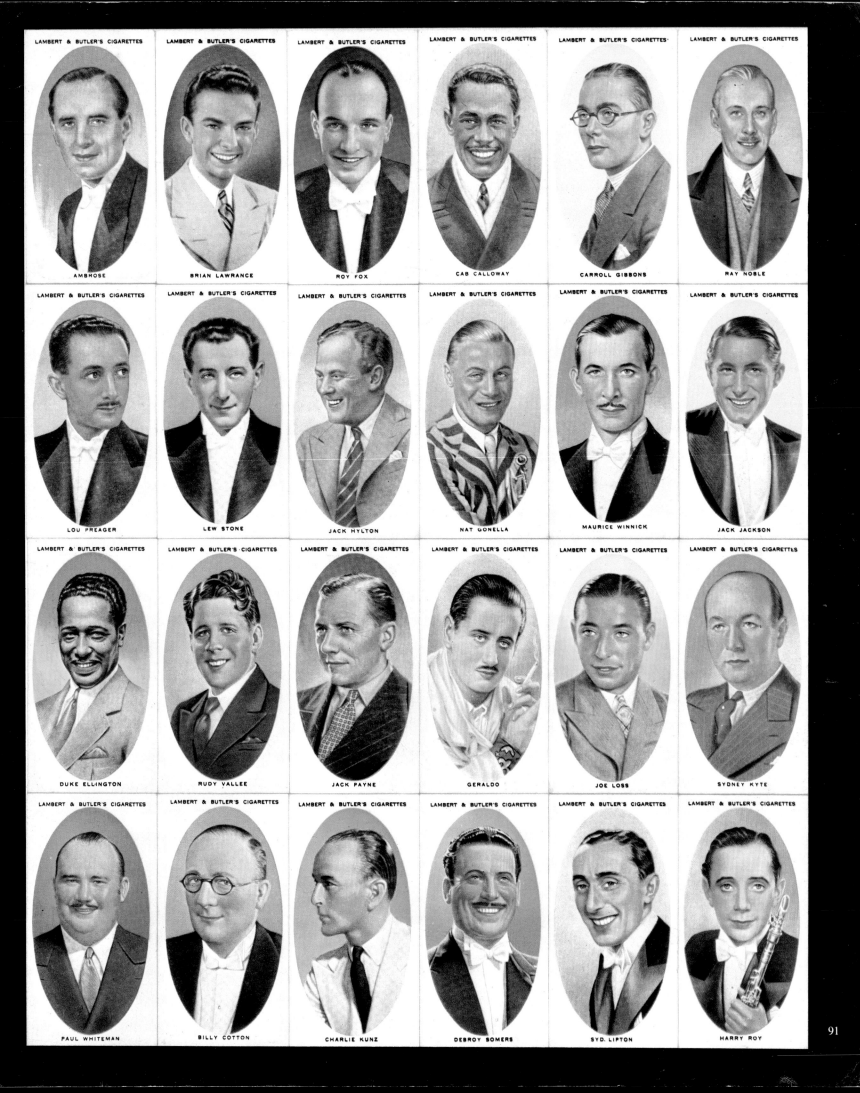

LAMBERT & BUTLER'S CIGARETTES — AMBROSE
LAMBERT & BUTLER'S CIGARETTES — BRIAN LAWRANCE
LAMBERT & BUTLER'S CIGARETTES — ROY FOX
LAMBERT & BUTLER'S CIGARETTES — CAB CALLOWAY
LAMBERT & BUTLER'S CIGARETTES — CARROLL GIBBONS
LAMBERT & BUTLER'S CIGARETTES — RAY NOBLE

LAMBERT & BUTLER'S CIGARETTES — LOU PREAGER
LAMBERT & BUTLER'S CIGARETTES — LEW STONE
LAMBERT & BUTLER'S CIGARETTES — JACK HYLTON
LAMBERT & BUTLER'S CIGARETTES — NAT GONELLA
LAMBERT & BUTLER'S CIGARETTES — MAURICE WINNICK
LAMBERT & BUTLER'S CIGARETTES — JACK JACKSON

LAMBERT & BUTLER'S CIGARETTES — DUKE ELLINGTON
LAMBERT & BUTLER'S CIGARETTES — RUDY VALLEE
LAMBERT & BUTLER'S CIGARETTES — JACK PAYNE
LAMBERT & BUTLER'S CIGARETTES — GERALDO
LAMBERT & BUTLER'S CIGARETTES — JOE LOSS
LAMBERT & BUTLER'S CIGARETTES — SYDNEY KYTE

LAMBERT & BUTLER'S CIGARETTES — PAUL WHITEMAN
LAMBERT & BUTLER'S CIGARETTES — BILLY COTTON
LAMBERT & BUTLER'S CIGARETTES — CHARLIE KUNZ
LAMBERT & BUTLER'S CIGARETTES — DEBROY SOMERS
LAMBERT & BUTLER'S CIGARETTES — SYD. LIPTON
LAMBERT & BUTLER'S CIGARETTES — HARRY ROY

CARRERAS
TURF RADIO CELEBRITIES 1950 B
SET OF 50
The only post-war set illustrated.
These cards were printed onto
the sliding 'tray' of the packet.

Collecting

People collect cards for a variety of reasons. Many will have started when a particular product they bought contained cards which had a certain appeal and were saved, perhaps to be stuck into a special album. Others discovered that a particular subject which interested them had been portrayed on cards and then collected or bought all the series concerned. Yet others seek to obtain cards as examples of printing techniques and art work, and many wish to have only one sample or 'type' card from each series rather than a complete set. Some are interested in a specific period or manufacturer and want only the cards representative of that era or company. Lastly, but by no means least, is the investment aspect because cards, like most collector's items, have tended to beat inflation in appreciating in value. Whatever the motives of collectors, they are all cartophilists and there are many thousands throughout the world.

There is, of course, the direct method of collecting cards from the cartons as they are issued, but this tends to be a rather hit and miss exercise, and cannot cover the cigarette cards from the golden age which we have illustrated in this book. Even where contemporary series are issued it is unlikely that an individual will buy the right packets to obtain a complete set. And all collectors remember the frustration of ending up with only part of a set and then being unable to obtain the missing cards that are needed. During the last 50 years, however, dealers in cards have appeared to help the collector. The company for which the author is a director, the London Cigarette Card Company of Somerton, Somerset, is able to supply most needs direct from stock, as the Company has millions of cards from thousands of different series. Dealers list their cards in catalogues which are usually published annually and most of them offer a mail order service throughout the world. The author's company details the oldest cigarette cards in its Catalogue Part I 1888 – 1919, between-the-war issues in its Catalogue Part II 1920 – 1940, and post-war cigarette cards, together with non-tobacco cards or trade issues of all periods, in its Catalogue Part III. The prices shown in dealers' catalogues are for cards in top condition.

The condition of the cards is, of course, of prime importance. A cracked piece of porcelain or a dog-eared stamp is usually valueless. The same applies to cigarette cards. Collectors are advised to ensure that the cards they buy are in the best possible condition – cracked, discoloured or grubby specimens should be avoided wherever possible. Having bought fine cards, the collector should ensure that they are stored in such a way that they will not deteriorate through humidity or handling. Ideally they should be kept at room temperature in a dry environment. For easy access and display without risk of marks caused by touch, the best method is to use special loose-leaf binders designed for the purpose. The London Cigarette Card Company, like most dealers, supply a range of albums and leaves to suit nearly every size of card.

Of course, prices of cards vary tremendously according to the series. As a rule, the older the cards, the more expensive they are. But this is only a very rough guide. It is really a question of supply and demand. The size of the print-run and the period which has elapsed since issue will affect the quantity of cards currently available. Demand will depend on the maker and the popularity of the subject. Some Wills, Players and Ogdens issues from before the First World War were produced in such large quantities that they are still commonplace today and this is reflected by the comparatively low prices which these series command. At the other end of the spectrum, certain recent trade issues have survived in only small quantities and fetch a high price.

Artificially high values for misprints are much less commonly found in cartophily than in philately; there are many freak cards, but they tend to be treated as curiosities rather than desirable items.

Card prices are still remarkably low in comparison with similar collectables. Complete sets of fifty pre-war cards are readily obtainable for a few pounds, the sort of sum a philatelist might expect to pay for just one stamp. Most post-war cards are a lot cheaper. A handful of really rare sets, invariably pre-1917, turn up only in auction and some of these can fetch four-figure sums, but bearing in mind that these are really the *crème de la crème*, such prices are by no means unrealistic. One thing is certain: there has been a ready market for cards in top condition for well over half a century. Interest in cartophily is continuing to grow, and the number of fine cards is limited. These are the conditions which create advancing prices and wise investment will reap its reward in the years to come.

Catalogues are, of course, extremely useful in that they provide the basic information needed by a collector – the manufacturer, series title, type of printing, the number of cards in a set, date of issue where known, and prices. These are complemented by reference books. There are handbooks which give additional details such as listing the subjects included in an unnumbered series so that the collector can determine which cards are missing from his own set, world indices covering foreign as well as British issues, trade indices and guide books on individual manufacturers. There is also a monthly magazine 'Cigarette Card News and Trade Chronicle' which offers collectors up-to-date information about new series, contains special articles by expert

contributors on various aspects of cartophily, research notes, readers' letters, auction information and free auction catalogues, free type cards of some new issues, advertisements and announcements, and lists of special offers.

For those readers who are considering starting a collection it is hoped that the cards and novelties we have illustrated and the accompanying text will act as an encouragement to get going. Cartophily is a rich and exciting subject and worthy of the growing number of collectors who join its ranks each year.

...JUVAMUS TUENDO

No. 13 (ARMY CO-OPERATION) SQUADRON, R.A.F.

POSSUNT QUIA POSSE VIDENTUR

No. 19 (FIGHTER) SQUADRON, R.A.F.

OCCIDENS ORIENSQUE

No. 203 (FLYING BOAT) SQUADRON, R.A.F.

EXCELLERE CONTENDE

No. 17 (FIGHTER) SQUADRON, R.A.F.

AIM SURE

No. 15 (BOMBER) SQUADRON, R.A.F.

...AGTER IN DIE LUG

No. 26 (ARMY CO-OPERATION) SQUADRON, R.A.F.

CAVETE: PRÆMONUI

No. 66 (FIGHTER) SQUADRON, R.A.F.

PER NOCTEM VOLAMUS

No. 9 (BOMBER) SQUADRON, R.A.F.

PREUX ET AUDACIEUX

No. 22 (TORPEDO BOMBER) SQUADRON, R.A.F.

IN FUTURUM VIDERE

No. 4 (ARMY CO-OPERATION) SQUADRON, R.A.F.

UNIFORMS OF THE TERRITORIAL ARMY

A SERIES OF 50

16

THE LOVAT SCOUTS, 1900

This mounted regiment of Scottish Highlanders was raised in Jan., 1900, by the 16th Lord Lovat. Recruits were chosen for their hardihood and powers of observation; they were equipped with sporting telescopes slung over the right shoulder, as shown in the picture. They took a prominent part in the South African War, first appearing in the Army List as "Lord Lovat's Corps—Mounted Infantry" and then as "Lovat's Scouts." They served during the Great War as dismounted troops, providing groups of highly-trained Corps Observers and snipers. The Lovat Scouts now form one regiment, the only one listed as scouts in the Army List. The picture shows a member of the Lovat Scouts during the South African War, with a typical ... farmhouse in the background.

UNIFORMS OF THE TERRITORIAL ARMY

A SERIES OF 50

17

ROYAL NORTH DEVON YEOMANRY (HUSSARS), 1908
Now: 96th (Royal Devon Yeomanry) Field Regiment, R.A.

The North Devon Yeomanry can claim a continuous existence since the formation on May 23rd, 1798, of a troop of Yeomen for local duties in Barnstaple and Bideford. Later they, with other Devon mounted units, were recruited to be ready to meet a possible French landing. The Regiment received the title "Royal" in 1856, and was trained and uniformed as a Hussar unit. After the Great War the Regiment, with the Royal 1st Devon Yeomanry, was converted to Artillery. The illustration is of our Chairman. It depicts him as he was 31 years ago. He served with this unit in the Great War. Bideford Bridge appears in the background.

UNIFORMS OF THE TERRITORIAL ARMY

A SERIES OF 50

18

EAST RIDING OF YORKSHIRE YEOMANRY, 1908
Now: East Riding of Yorkshire Yeomanry Royal Armoured Corps

Raised in 1902 by the late Lord Wenlock as Imperial Yeomanry, this unit was recruited in the East Riding. During the Great War two regiments were raised, and saw service in France, Egypt and Palestine. In 1922 the unit was reconstituted as the 26th Armoured Car Company, The Royal Tank Corps. In 1939 it again adopted a cavalry role as a mechanized cavalry unit, which is incorporated in the Royal Armoured Corps. We show a trooper in the uniform of the pre-War Yeomanry period. In the background are the Dock offices and Wilberforce Memorial, Kingston-upon-Hull, in which city the unit's H.Q.'s are now situated.

UNIFORMS OF THE TERRITORIAL ARMY

A SERIES OF 50

19

GLAMORGANSHIRE R.G.A., 1908
Now: Glamorgan Heavy Regiment, R.A.

This regiment was raised in Cardiff and Swansea in 1859 as the Glamorganshire Artillery Volunteers. During the Volunteer period the unit was chiefly armed with 40-pounder and 64-pounder guns, but by the time the Territorial Force was formed it had received the 6-inch gun shown in the background. At this time the unit became the Glamorganshire Royal Garrison Artillery. During the War of 1914-18 the unit comprised ten heavy batteries for service in France and two A.A. batteries for home defence. The latter took a prominent part in beating off the Zeppelin raid of Sept. 7th, 1915. In 1908 it was renamed the Glamorgan Heavy Regiment, R.A. (T.A.). The picture shows a gunner in pre-War uniform.

UNIFORMS OF THE TERRITORIAL ARMY

A SERIES OF 50

20

6TH BN. THE NORTHUMBERLAND FUSILIERS, 1908
Now: 43rd Bn. (6th Bn. The Royal Northumberland Fusiliers) Royal Tank Regiment

This battalion owes its origin to the Newcastle Rifle Club, which in 1860 formed a unit under the title of the 1st Newcastle-on-Tyne Rifle Volunteers. The uniform was changed from dark grey to scarlet in 1872, and in ... was again changed to conform with that of the County Regiment—the 5th Foot. The Battalion went to the Great War as part of the 50th (Northumbrian) Division, going overseas on April 20th, 1915. The ... was converted into the 43rd Bn., ... Tank Regiment on Nov. 1st, ... We show an officer in full dress (1908) with the Keep and Black Gate, Newcastle-upon-Tyne, in the background.

10TH BATTALION LONDON REGIMENT, T.A.

Index and Acknowledgments

All cards and novelties have been reproduced approximately the same size except where indicated. Dates of publication relate to first publication and may not represent the date of the examples shown.

*The illustrations of mixed novelty items
(on pages 47, 48, 49, 51, 52, & 53)
have not been included in the index.*

Acknowledgments

The publishers would like to thank:
M. A. Murray of Murray Cards International for his kind help in allowing us to photograph his set of Clowns & Circus Artistes by Taddy illustrated on page 15.

Imperial Tobacco Limited for their permission to publish examples from cards issued by Ogdens, Lambert & Butler, Edwards Ringer & Bigg, Churchman, Franklyn Davey, Wills, and Players.

Carreras Rothmans Limited for their permission to publish examples from Famous Film Stars 1939 (R J Lea) reproduced by permission of John Sinclair Ltd., Beauties of The Cinema 1939 (Rothmans) reproduced by permission of Rothmans of Pall Mall Ltd., and Turf Radio Celebrities 1950 (Carreras) reproduced by permission of Carreras Ltd.

British-American Tobacco Company Limited for their agreement that we may reproduce by permission of Ardath Tobacco Co. Ltd. the Empire Flying Boat 1938, Film Stars & Radio Stars 1935, Who Is This? 1936, and Cricket Tennis & Golf Celebrities 1935.

The publishers have taken every effort to clear other copyright material.

Further Reading

Dealers in cigarette cards stock and sell most of the literature available for collectors.

The most useful general introduction to the subject is Dorothy Bagnall's *Collecting Cigarette Cards* published by the London Cigarette Card Company.

The Company is also the publisher of
Cigarette Card News & Trade Card Chronicle
a monthly journal with subscribers all over the world.

A simple price code has been used to give the reader a guide as to the retail price of sets, in good condition, at the time of publication. The letters indicate the price range shown, and have been placed after the issue date in the captions to illustrations.

A Under £5

B £5 to £20

C £20 to £50

D £50 to £100

E Over £100